The East African
COOKBOOK

The East African
COOKBOOK

SHEREEN JOG

Published in 2020 by Struik Lifestyle,
an imprint of Penguin Random House
South Africa (Pty) Ltd
Company Reg. No. 1953/000441/07
The Estuaries, 4 Oxbow Crescent, Century Avenue,
Century City 7441, Cape Town, South Africa
PO Box 1144, Cape Town, 8000, South Africa

www.penguinrandomhouse.co.za

PUBLISHER: Beverley Dodd
MANAGING EDITOR: Cecilia Barfield
EDITOR: Bronwen Maynier
DESIGNER: Helen Henn
PROOFREADER and INDEXER: Joy Nel
PHOTOGRAPHER: Warren Heath
PHOTOGRAPHER (pages 3, 6): Julius Moshiro
STYLIST: Caro Alberts
ASSISTANTS: Claire Ellen Van Rooyen and
Kaylen Rolfe

Reproduction by Studio Repro and Hirt & Carter Cape (Pty) Ltd
Printed and bound in China by 1010 Printing International Ltd

ISBN 978-1-43231-034-9

MIX
Paper from
responsible sources
FSC® C016973

To my husband, who believed in my abilities and who
encouraged, supported and motivated me every little step
of the way. Thank you for treating my hobby and passion for
cooking with as much respect as your own career.
And for that, I love you so very deeply.

CONTENTS

ACKNOWLEDGEMENTS

I would like to thank my mother, my number one fan and perpetual support system, who originally taught me the basics of cooking when I was just a young girl. Her constant support through this five-year-long cookbook journey cannot be put into words, and the value she brought to the finished product — by reading the manuscript, tasting my dishes, looking after my infants while I worked, and so much more — is something for which I will always be grateful.

I would also like to thank my friends Afzaa and Nikita for giving me the opportunity to develop my cooking skills by being my most constructive critics and my first guinea pigs outside of my family; as well as my friends Aya, Beejal, Hetal, Hanna, Jolita (Jo), Koonti, Lise and Sabrina for motivating me and supporting me every step of the way, right to the end.

I must also thank most deeply my brother-in-law Tamish and his wife Priyanka for all their assistance in the final stages of this book, from ensuring that I met my deadlines to supporting me in every way they could. I am ever so grateful to have such amazing friends and family in my life, without whose support this book would have remained no more than a dream.

Dar es Salaam city view

INTRODUCTION

In the early nineteenth century, people of Indian origin started arriving on the beautiful, undeveloped shores of East Africa as traders. Slightly later in the century, there was a further influx of Indians, brought by the British to work as indentured labourers in different parts of East Africa. Stationed in Kenya, Uganda and Tanzania, some worked on the railway lines, while others became traders and shopkeepers. Living among the local communities and tribes, these Indians chose to become East African citizens. Intermarriage and cross-communal bonding resulted in the current ecosystem: a region that is a beautiful amalgamation of Indian and Arab influences on language, cuisine and values.

My great-grandfather made his way over to Tanga, Tanzania, from Diu, India, in the 1890s in a sailboat. For the last five generations, my family has created and passed down recipes that truly depict what East African cuisine is all about: the freshest local ingredients, cooked using traditional methods, creating scintillating flavours and wholesome food. Food is a huge part of East African life. The dinner table is a sacred place, and families traditionally eat meals together daily. Mealtimes are something the whole family looks forward to, as food brings them closer and creates beautiful memories and moments.

The traditional East African favourites in this book have evolved over the years to account for the growth of our region and the various additional cultures we have imbibed. East Africa has one of the world's fastest-growing populations, and the new younger generation is worldly wise and thoroughly modern. Their exposure to global trends means that a new wave of locally enjoyed cuisine is gaining in popularity across the region. The recipe selection in this book is therefore as modern as it is traditional, as healthy as it is wholesome, as organic as it is contemporary. It is my opportunity to share with you what we love and enjoy as East Africans. Combining the fruit of the highlands, the spices of Zanzibar, the vegetables of the rich and fertile soil, and meat and seafood untouched by genetic modification, East African cuisine is something everyone can enjoy and adapt.

'All that stuff you thought you wanted, the most jaw dropping moments, it's here.'

Anthony Bourdain on visiting Tanzania in 2014

Chickpea and roasted red bell pepper salad

Salads

CHICKPEA AND ROASTED RED BELL PEPPER SALAD

1 tsp olive oil
1 red bell pepper
50 g rocket leaves
1 cup tinned chickpeas
1 red onion, thinly sliced
¼ cup chopped fresh coriander
¼ tsp salt
50 g flaked almonds

DRESSING
3 Tbsp orange juice
1 Tbsp lemon or lime juice
½ tsp dried red chilli flakes
¼ tsp cayenne pepper (optional)

1. Preheat the oven to 220 °C. Grease an ovenproof dish or baking tray with the olive oil and roast the bell pepper for 20 minutes or until it starts to char, turning it occasionally. Set the bell pepper aside to cool for 5 minutes before deseeding and chopping into even cubes.

2. Wash the rocket leaves and pat dry with paper towel. Trim the stems if necessary.

3. Drain and rinse the chickpeas to remove excess brine.

4. In a mixing bowl, combine the chickpeas, red onion, chopped roasted bell pepper, rocket leaves, coriander and salt.

5. Combine the dressing ingredients, pour over the salad and mix well. Transfer to a serving dish.

6. Place a small frying pan over medium heat and dry-roast the flaked almonds for approximately 1 minute, tossing frequently to avoid burning. Sprinkle the roasted almonds over the salad when ready to serve.

Serves 4

Going for the healthy option doesn't necessarily mean giving up on satisfying your taste buds. This salad is a perfect example of that, with its mild chilli and seared chicken combined with protein-rich maharage (East African red kidney beans), a staple in the local diet. Enjoy without remorse!

CHICKEN SALAD WITH MAHARAGE

2 tsp olive oil
1 yellow bell pepper
1 cup dried red kidney beans or
    1 x 400 g tin red kidney beans
4 cups water
½ tsp salt
¼ cup halved cherry tomatoes
2 cups chopped lettuce
1 Tbsp chopped fresh basil, plus extra
    for garnishing
1 Tbsp chopped fresh parsley
1 tsp lemon or lime juice

MARINATED CHICKEN
2 deboned chicken breasts
1 tsp lemon or lime juice
1 red chilli, finely chopped (optional)
1 tsp garlic paste
1 tsp ginger paste
¼ tsp salt
1 tsp olive oil

1. First prepare the marinated chicken. Place the chicken breasts in a bowl and rub with the lemon or lime juice, chilli (if using), garlic paste, ginger paste and salt. Cover the bowl and leave to marinate in the fridge for 30 minutes.
2. In a frying pan, heat the olive oil and sear the marinated chicken breasts over medium heat for approximately 3 minutes on each side. Cut the chicken breasts lengthwise into pieces about 2.5 cm thick.
3. Preheat the oven to 220 °C. Grease an ovenproof dish or baking tray with 1 tsp of the olive oil and roast the bell pepper for 20 minutes or until it starts to char, turning it occasionally. Set the bell pepper aside to cool for 5 minutes before deseeding and chopping into even cubes.
4. If using dried kidney beans, soak them for at least 4 hours, drain and rinse thoroughly, and then place in a saucepan with the water and ¼ tsp of the salt. Boil for approximately 25 minutes over high heat (check frequently to avoid overcooking). Drain and set aside. If using tinned kidney beans, drain the liquid and rinse the beans to remove excess salt.
5. In a mixing bowl, combine the kidney beans, chopped roasted bell pepper, cherry tomatoes, lettuce, basil, parsley, lemon or lime juice, and the remaining ¼ tsp salt and 1 tsp olive oil.
6. Toss the salad and transfer to a serving bowl. Place the chicken pieces on top and garnish with extra chopped fresh basil.

Serves 4

Cucumber, called tango in Kiswahili, is mostly enjoyed freshly peeled and sprinkled with lime, salt and red chilli powder. You will frequently see it being sold on the streets as a light snack. This particular recipe is a creation of mine using local, fresh and easily available produce, and has become a lunch favourite paired with a light protein main.

CUCUMBER, PEAR AND MINT SALAD

1 medium cucumber
1 pear
3 spring onions, chopped
½ white onion, chopped
2 Tbsp chopped fresh mint
fresh mint leaves and cucumber ribbons for garnishing

DRESSING
2 tsp distilled white vinegar
1 Tbsp olive oil
2 tsp lemon or lime juice
salt to taste

1. Peel the cucumber, scoop out the seeds and chop into 2.5 cm cubes.
2. Peel the pear and chop into matching cubes.
3. In a mixing bowl, combine the cucumber, pear, spring onions, white onion and chopped mint.
4. Use a whisk to combine the dressing ingredients well, then pour over the salad.
5. Transfer to a serving bowl and garnish with fresh mint leaves and cucumber ribbons.

Serves 2

Mango trees are common in backyards across Tanzania. I spent many an afternoon in my childhood picking the fruit in season. Mangoes are used at every stage of their life and in every form imaginable, from freshly cut and freshly squeezed to dried and pickled. A favourite way of serving mango, and one you'll see on the roadside, is almost ripe, cut into cubes and sprinkled with red chilli powder. If your family loves tasty sides with every meal as much as mine does, this salsa makes an excellent addition to a protein-based main course.

GINGER AND MANGO SALSA
WITH TOMATO, ONION AND CORIANDER

3 large mangoes, chopped
2 tomatoes, chopped, or 200 g cherry
    tomatoes, quartered
1 red or white onion, chopped
3 Tbsp chopped fresh coriander
½ Tbsp grated fresh ginger (grate with the skin on)

DRESSING
1 Tbsp olive oil
1 Tbsp lemon or lime juice
¼ tsp chopped fresh red chilli (optional)
¼ tsp salt

1. Place the mangoes, tomatoes, onion, coriander and ginger in a mixing bowl.
2. Use a whisk to combine the dressing ingredients well, then pour over the salad.
3. Toss well and transfer to a serving dish.

Serves 2–4

Biringanya, or aubergine, is one of a relatively limited variety of vegetables commonly used in East African cuisine. Originally brought over from India, aubergine is favoured for its versatility, and is used extensively in salads and curries.

ROASTED BIRINGANYA AND TOMATO SALAD

1 tsp cumin seeds
1 tsp coriander seeds
olive oil
2 medium aubergines, halved
10 Roma or cherry tomatoes, halved

¼ tsp salt
¼ tsp dried red chilli flakes
pinch of red chilli powder
1 Tbsp chopped fresh parsley

1. Place a small frying pan over medium heat and dry-toast the cumin and coriander seeds for approximately 2 minutes or until fragrant, tossing frequently. Grind the toasted seeds in a pestle and mortar, then set aside.
2. Preheat the oven to 220 °C. Grease an ovenproof dish or baking tray with 1 tsp olive oil and line with baking paper. Roast the halved aubergines and tomatoes for 20–25 minutes. The flesh of the aubergine should appear cooked and be soft to the touch; the tomatoes should begin to appear wilted and wrinkled. Allow the aubergines to cool to room temperature before cutting into medium-sized cubes.
3. Place the roasted cubed aubergine and roasted tomatoes in a mixing bowl. Handle gently to avoid mashing.
4. Add the toasted crushed cumin and coriander seeds. Drizzle over 1 Tbsp olive oil and season with the salt, chilli flakes and chilli powder. Toss well and transfer to a serving plate.
5. Garnish with the chopped fresh parsley before serving.

Serves 2–4

Avocado, called parachichi in Kiswahili, is available at most roadside fruit stalls and is enjoyed by nearly every Tanzanian. Strawberry farming is on the rise in Kenya, due to a more favourable climate, making growing and harvesting easier than in other places across the region. A modern blend of traditional ingredients, this recently created recipe is a favourite with the younger generations of East Africans and is an excellent example of contemporary East African cuisine.

ROASTED WALNUT, AVOCADO AND STRAWBERRY SALAD

100 g walnuts
3 ripe avocados, diced
1 cup halved strawberries

DRESSING
2 Tbsp olive oil
¼ tsp Dijon mustard
½ tsp honey
1 Tbsp red wine vinegar
¼ tsp dried red chilli flakes
¼ tsp salt

1. Place a small frying pan over medium heat and dry-roast the walnuts for approximately 1 minute, tossing frequently to ensure they do not char. Set aside.
2. Place the avocados and strawberries in a mixing bowl.
3. Use a whisk to combine the dressing ingredients well, then pour over the fresh ingredients. Stir gently and transfer to a serving platter.
4. Add the roasted walnuts just before serving.

Serves 4

Roasted walnut, avocado and strawberry salad

Minestrone soup

Soups

Found on every continental restaurant menu in the region, this local adaption of the famous Italian soup is so well known that most locals don't know its origin and believe it to be East African! Pronounced 'mini-stroni supu'.

MINESTRONE SOUP

1 Tbsp butter
5 garlic cloves, roughly chopped
8 tomatoes, peeled and chopped, or
    1 x 400 g tin chopped peeled tomatoes
2 red onions, chopped
6 cups water
1 chicken or vegetable stock cube or
    1 heaped Tbsp stock powder

1 carrot, peeled and cubed
1 potato, peeled and cubed
1 Tbsp tomato purée or paste
1 celery stalk, chopped
½ baby marrow, chopped
1 tsp coarsely ground black pepper
½ tsp salt
fresh coriander for garnishing

1. In a large saucepan, melt the butter over medium heat and sauté the garlic for 30 seconds.
2. Stir in the tomatoes and onions, cover the pan with a lid and simmer for approximately 3 minutes.
3. Add the water followed by the stock cube or powder and give it a good stir.
4. Add the carrot and potato, and simmer for 15–18 minutes over medium to high heat.
5. Add the remaining ingredients, except the coriander, and simmer for 5 minutes.
6. Garnish with fresh coriander and serve with a side of garlic bread.

Serves 4

This is an East African adaption of the classic tomato soup, which has been modified to be slightly spicier with an underlying paprika and jalapeño base. It achieves the same 'feel good' result and is a family favourite when we go up to our holiday home in the Usambara Mountains, to chilly Lushoto!

TOMATO SOUP WITH ROASTED RED BELL PEPPER

1 red bell pepper
½ Tbsp olive oil
½ Tbsp butter
5 garlic cloves, chopped
½ cup chopped celery
1 onion, chopped
8 tomatoes, peeled and chopped, or
    4 x 400 g tins chopped peeled tomatoes
2 Tbsp tomato purée or paste
¼ tsp paprika

1 red jalapeño chilli pepper, chopped (optional)
½ tsp ground black pepper
½ tsp salt
4 cups vegetable or chicken stock (made with 1 stock
    cube or 1 Tbsp stock powder)
2 Tbsp cooking cream (such as Nestlé Dessert &
    Cooking Cream)

1. Preheat the oven to 220 °C. Rub the bell pepper with the olive oil and place on a baking tray or piece of baking paper. Roast until the bell pepper starts to char or black spots appear. Set aside to cool for 5 minutes before deseeding and chopping.

2. In a large saucepan, melt the butter over medium heat and sauté the garlic for 30 seconds.

3. Add the celery and onion, and sauté for approximately 2 minutes.

4. Add the tomatoes, tomato purée or paste, paprika, jalapeño chilli pepper (if using), black pepper, salt and chopped roasted bell pepper. Mix well.

5. Stir in the stock, cover the saucepan with a lid and cook for 20 minutes over medium to high heat. Remove from the heat and allow to cool to room temperature.

6. Strain the soup, reserving the liquid, and pour the vegetables into a blender. Blend on low speed until smooth. Pour the blended mixture back into the saucepan with the reserved liquid, add the cream and stir well. Simmer over low heat for 2 minutes and serve.

Serves 2–4

POTATO AND LEEK SOUP

1 Tbsp butter
5 garlic cloves, chopped
2 leeks (white part only), chopped
1 medium celery stalk, chopped
5 potatoes, peeled and cubed
½ Tbsp ground black pepper

2 cups chicken or vegetable stock (made with
   1 stock cube or 1 Tbsp stock powder)
¼ cup cooking cream (such as Nestlé Dessert &
   Cooking Cream)
salt to taste

1. In a large saucepan, melt the butter over medium to high heat and sauté the garlic for approximately 15 seconds, making sure the garlic does not brown.
2. Add the leeks and sauté for approximately 2 minutes or until they start to soften.
3. Add the celery, potatoes, black pepper and chicken or vegetable stock. Cover the saucepan with a lid and bring to the boil. Boil for approximately 20 minutes or until the potatoes are cooked through. Turn off the heat.
4. Bring the soup to room temperature, then transfer to a blender. Blend for approximately 30 seconds on medium speed until well combined and smooth, then pour back into the saucepan.
5. Add the cream, season with salt and simmer for 2 minutes over medium heat. If the soup appears too thick, add some water and season with extra salt and black pepper.
6. Serve with toasted bruschetta or croutons.

Serves 4

This is an ideal winter soup, healthy and oh so nutritious. It has a creamy texture and is so filling and delicious with a side of garlic bread. It is my all-time favourite and I've made it on each of the three continents on which I've lived!

VELVETY VEGETABLE SOUP

1 Tbsp butter
5 garlic cloves, roughly chopped
1 cup fresh or tinned peas
1 cup chopped green beans
8 tomatoes, chopped
4 red onions, chopped

2 medium carrots, peeled and chopped
2 medium potatoes, peeled and chopped
2 tsp tomato purée or paste
½ tsp ground black pepper
1 tsp salt
6 cups water

1. In a large saucepan, melt the butter over medium heat and sauté the garlic for approximately 15 seconds.
2. Add all the vegetables, tomato purée or paste, black pepper and salt. Mix well.
3. Add the water and bring to the boil. Partially cover the saucepan with a lid and boil for approximately 25 minutes. Turn off the heat.
4. Bring the soup to room temperature, then transfer to a blender. Blend for 15 seconds on medium speed, then pour back into the saucepan and reheat for 1 minute before serving.

NOTE: If using tinned peas, add them towards the end to avoid overcooking.

Serves 4

Served in every roadside bar and restaurant in Tanzania, chicken soup made with seasonal vegetables cures hangovers and illness, and acts as an icebreaker for new friends at the beginning of a meal every time. It is usually served with a side of freshly cut pili pili mbuzi (a close cousin of the habanero chilli pepper) and lemon wedges to taste.

SUPU YA KUKU [CHICKEN SOUP]

1 Tbsp butter
5 large or 10 small garlic cloves, roughly chopped
10 whole black peppercorns
1 large red onion, halved
1 large tomato, halved
4 chicken thighs, skinned
6 cups water

1 cup roughly chopped cabbage
1 small celery stalk, halved
½ cup fresh coriander leaves with stems
1 carrot, peeled and halved
1 potato, peeled
1 tsp salt
½ green bell pepper, deseeded

1. In a large saucepan, melt the butter over medium heat and sauté the garlic and black peppercorns for 30 seconds.
2. Add the onion and tomato halves, and sauté for 1 minute.
3. Add the chicken thighs, mix well and pour in the water.
4. Add the cabbage, celery, coriander, carrot, whole potato and salt. Partially cover the saucepan with a lid and bring to the boil. Boil for approximately 25 minutes over medium to high heat.
5. Add the bell pepper and boil, uncovered, for approximately 5 minutes.
6. Strain the soup into a serving bowl, adding only the chicken thighs back into the clear soup.

Serves 4

Supu ya kuku (chicken soup)

Mchuzi wa nyama (beef curry)

Meat

Made in every home, Swahili beef curry is prepared using a blend of Arabic and Indian spices, and is typically served with the slightly sticky and aromatic mbeya rice that is loved throughout the region.

MCHUZI WA NYAMA [BEEF CURRY]

3 Tbsp oil
8 whole cloves
8 whole black peppercorns
1 large red onion, chopped
1 whole fresh red or green chilli
1 Tbsp garlic paste
½ Tbsp ginger paste
4 large tomatoes, grated, or 2 x 410 g tins
    tomato purée
½ tsp ground turmeric
1 tsp ground cumin

1 Tbsp curry powder
1 tsp ground coriander
½ tsp salt
½ tsp red chilli powder or cayenne pepper or paprika
500 g beef fillet, cut into 5 cm cubes (you can also use
    mutton or lamb)
2 cups water
1 tsp garam masala
2 Tbsp lemon or lime juice
¼ cup fresh coriander

1. In a large saucepan, heat the oil over high heat and add the whole cloves and black peppercorns. Let the spices crackle for 15 seconds, then add the onion and whole chilli, and sauté until the onion starts to brown.
2. Lower the heat and add the garlic paste, ginger paste, tomatoes, turmeric, cumin, curry powder, ground coriander, salt and red chilli powder, cayenne pepper or paprika. Stir and cover the pan with a lid. Simmer for approximately 3 minutes.
3. Add the beef and combine well.
4. Add the water and cook, covered, over medium heat for 20 minutes.
5. Add the garam masala and lemon or lime juice, and simmer for approximately 3 minutes. Remove from the heat and garnish with the fresh coriander.
6. Serve with steamed rice or chapattis.

NOTE: Garam masala is a combination of ground cumin, coriander, cinnamon, cardamom, black pepper and cloves.

Serves 2

MCHUZI WA KEEMA
[BEEF MINCE CURRY WITH PEAS AND POTATOES]

250 g beef mince
3 Tbsp oil
1 medium cinnamon stick
3 whole cloves
3 whole black peppercorns
3 cardamom pods
1 red onion, finely chopped
1 tsp ginger paste
2 tsp garlic paste
6 large tomatoes, grated
1 Tbsp tomato purée or paste
¼ tsp ground turmeric

2 tsp ground cumin
1 Tbsp curry powder
¼ tsp red chilli powder or cayenne pepper
1 tsp ground coriander
¼ cup chopped fresh coriander, plus extra
  for garnishing
1 potato, peeled and chopped into 2.5 cm cubes
½ cup fresh or tinned peas
½ tsp salt
1 cup water
2 tsp lemon or lime juice

1. Wash the beef mince and place in a strainer to drain the excess water.
2. In a large saucepan, heat the oil over medium heat and sauté the cinnamon stick, whole cloves, black peppercorns and cardamom pods for 1 minute, allowing the spices to crackle.
3. Add the onion and sauté until it starts to brown.
4. Add the ginger paste and garlic paste, followed by the grated tomatoes and tomato purée or paste. Give it a good stir.
5. Add the turmeric, cumin, curry powder, red chilli powder or cayenne pepper, ground coriander and chopped fresh coriander. Combine well using a spatula, then cover the saucepan with a lid and simmer for 3–4 minutes over medium heat.
6. Add the beef mince, potato, peas, salt and water, and cook, covered, for a further 20 minutes.
7. Add the lemon or lime juice just before taking the saucepan off the heat. Give it a good stir and garnish with extra chopped fresh coriander.

NOTES: If using tinned peas, rather add them towards the end of cooking to avoid mashing them.
You can substitute the whole spices for ground spices, in which case skip step 2 and just add to the pan along with the grated tomatoes.

Serves 2

MCHUZI WA KABABU [LAMB KOFTA CURRY]

LAMB KOFTAS
250 g lamb mince (you can also
    use beef mince)
1 tsp garlic paste
½ tsp ginger paste
1 tsp ground coriander
¼ tsp ground turmeric
¼ tsp red chilli powder
¼ tsp salt
¼ cup chopped fresh coriander

CURRY
2 Tbsp oil
4 whole cloves
4 whole black peppercorns
3 cardamom pods
1 red onion, finely chopped
5 large tomatoes, grated
1 tsp ground cumin
1 tsp ground coriander
1 tsp curry powder
1 tsp garam masala

¼ tsp ground turmeric
1 tsp garlic paste
½ tsp ginger paste
1 Tbsp tomato purée or paste
½ tsp lemon or lime juice
¼ tsp salt
1 cup water
fresh coriander and lemon zest
    for garnishing

1. First make the lamb koftas. Wash the lamb mince and place in a strainer to drain any excess water. Transfer to a mixing bowl and add the rest of the ingredients. Combine using a spatula. Roll the mixture into smooth 7.5 cm balls using the palms of your hands.

2. To make the curry, heat the oil in a large saucepan over medium heat and add the cloves, black peppercorns and cardamom pods. Sauté for 1 minute or until the spices start to crackle.

3. Add the onion and sauté until it just starts to brown.

4. Add the rest of the ingredients, except the water and garnish. Mix well, cover the pan with a lid and simmer for approximately 3 minutes.

5. Add the water and simmer for a further 5–7 minutes.

6. Now gently drop the meatballs into the curry, spacing them to make turning the meatballs while cooking easier. Cook, covered, over low heat for approximately 8 minutes, gently turning the meatballs after 4 minutes to allow for even cooking.

7. Garnish with fresh coriander and lemon zest and serve with steamed rice.

NOTE: Meatballs larger than 5 cm are easier to handle. Covering the saucepan will ensure the meatballs cook through, especially if they are large.

Serves 2

Mkate mayai in Kiswahili means egg bread, but interestingly there is no bread in the recipe. The traditional way of eating this dish is with a side of bread or typical East African chapattis (see page 134).

MKATE MAYAI [BAKED MINCE MEAT TOPPED WITH EGGS]

500 g beef mince
3 Tbsp oil
2 red onions, chopped
3 large tomatoes, grated
2 tsp garlic paste
2 tsp ginger paste
2 Tbsp tomato purée or paste
¼ tsp ground turmeric
1 tsp red chilli powder
1 tsp ground cumin
1 tsp ground coriander

1 tsp curry powder
½ tsp garam masala
1 tsp salt
¼ cup water
1 tsp lemon or lime juice
4 large eggs

1. Wash the beef mince and place in a strainer to drain any excess water.
2. Heat the oil in a frying pan over medium heat and sauté the onions until golden brown.
3. Add the tomatoes, give it a good stir, then add the garlic paste, ginger paste, tomato purée or paste, turmeric, red chilli powder, cumin, coriander, curry powder, garam masala and salt. Stir well and simmer for 2–3 minutes.
4. Add the beef mince and water, and simmer until the mince is cooked but not dry. If the mince appears too dry, add 2 Tbsp water. Remove from the heat and stir in the lemon or lime juice.
5. Preheat the oven to 160 °C. Spoon the cooked mince into an ovenproof dish and crack the eggs on top, spacing them evenly. Place the dish in the oven and bake for 10–12 minutes or until the eggs appear cooked through.
6. Serve with chapattis or bread of your choice.

Serves 4

I like to describe pilau as a flavoursome rice, made using five locally harvested spices: cardamom, clove, cinnamon, black peppercorns and cumin. Kachumbari is a fresh tomato and onion salad that is popular in East Africa, particularly in Kenya, but also in Tanzania, Rwanda, Burundi and Uganda. This traditional dish is enjoyed across the region and is usually served as a celebration meal. Pilau takes time, but is well worth the effort.

BEEF PILAU WITH KACHUMBARI

500 g beef fillet, cut into 5 cm cubes
1 Tbsp salt
2 tsp ginger paste
3 tsp garlic paste
2 tsp green chilli paste
5 cups water
¼ cup oil
1 Tbsp whole cumin seeds
1 cinnamon stick
4 whole cloves
4 cardamom pods
6 whole black peppercorns
1 large red onion, finely chopped

1 large tomato, grated
2 cups long-grain or basmati rice, soaked for 30 minutes
¼ tsp ground coriander
¼ tsp ground cumin
handful of chopped fresh coriander

KACHUMBARI

1 red onion, diced
1 large tomato, diced
1 Tbsp lemon or lime juice
salt to taste
pinch of red chilli powder

1. Place the beef in a small saucepan and rub with ¼ Tbsp of the salt and 1 tsp each of the ginger paste, garlic paste and green chilli paste. Leave to marinate for a minimum of 15–20 minutes.
2. Add the water to the marinated beef and boil over medium to high heat for 20 minutes or until the beef is cooked through. Strain the beef, reserving the stock.
3. Heat the oil in a large saucepan over medium heat and add the cumin seeds, cinnamon, cloves, cardamom and black peppercorns. Allow the spices to crackle for approximately 1 minute.
4. Add the onion to the spices and sauté until pink and translucent.
5. Add the tomato and the remaining ginger paste, garlic paste and green chilli paste. Stir and leave to simmer for approximately 2 minutes.
6. Lower the heat and add the cooked beef. Stir well.
7. Drain the rice and add it to the saucepan along with all the reserved beef stock, the remaining salt, the ground coriander and cumin, and the chopped fresh coriander. Cover the saucepan with a lid and cook over medium heat for 15–20 minutes or until the rice is cooked and all the stock has been absorbed.
8. To make the kachumbari, mix all the ingredients in a bowl and serve as an accompaniment to the pilau.

Serves 4

Beef pilau with kachumbari

Although it shares a name with the more common European meatloaf, this East African variant originated within the Ismaili Muslim sub-sect, which has a strong presence in East Africa. This is a wholesome, filling dish loved by everyone who has ever tried it. The recipe remains closely guarded within families and is not generally available to 'outsiders'.

EAST AFRICAN 'MEATLOAF'
[BAKED BEEF AND EGG ROLL WITH SPICY TOMATO SAUCE]

400 g beef mince
1 tsp garlic paste
½ tsp ginger paste
¼ tsp salt
1 tsp red chilli powder
¼ tsp curry powder
¼ tsp ground turmeric

¼ tsp garam masala
1½ Tbsp oil
1 large egg, beaten

SPICY TOMATO SAUCE
2 Tbsp oil
¼ cup tomato purée or paste

¼ tsp ground turmeric
¼ tsp red chilli powder
1 tsp garlic paste
½ tsp ginger paste
¼ tsp salt
¼ cup water
2 tsp lemon or lime juice

1. Preheat the oven to 230 °C.
2. In a mixing bowl, combine the mince, garlic paste, ginger paste, salt, red chilli powder, curry powder, turmeric and garam masala. Mix well and form into a large ball using your hands.
3. Heat ½ Tbsp of the oil in a frying pan and pour in the beaten egg. Cook as you would an omelette and set aside.
4. On a piece of 25 x 25 cm aluminium foil, flatten the mince mixture with your hands to form a circle at least 5 cm larger in circumference than your omelette. You can trim the omelette if needs be using a knife or kitchen scissors.
5. Place the omelette on top of the flattened mince and use the foil to fold each side inwards to form an oblong shape. Make sure the omelette is completely covered.
6. Grease an ovenproof dish or meatloaf pan with the remaining oil. Lift the mince roll from the foil with your hands and place it gently in the greased dish. Bake for approximately 25 minutes.
7. To make the spicy tomato sauce, heat the oil in a wide saucepan or skillet over medium heat.
8. Add the tomato purée or paste and stir in the turmeric, red chilli powder, garlic paste, ginger paste and salt. Cover the saucepan or skillet with a lid and simmer for approximately 1 minute.
9. Add the water and mix well. Simmer, covered, for approximately 3 minutes.
10. Add the lemon or lime juice and simmer for another minute. Remove from the heat.
11. Place the baked mince roll in the saucepan and coat with the sauce.
12. Slice the roll and serve with French fries or steamed veggies.

Serves 2

Beef threaded on skewers is known as mishkaki in Kiswahili, and it is a traditional Tanzanian way of cooking cubed meat on the grill. Served on the streets of the country's cities and towns, in restaurants and in cafés along scenic highways, these are a must-have at backyard barbecues on Sunday afternoons. I have enhanced the flavour in my version using various ground spices for an absolutely mouth-watering effect!

MISHKAKI [BEEF SKEWERS]

1 kg beef fillet, cut into 5 cm cubes (you can also
   use rump)
2 red onions, chopped into 5 cm cubes
2 Tbsp garlic paste
1 Tbsp ginger paste
¼ tsp ground turmeric
½ tsp red chilli powder or cayenne pepper or paprika
1 tsp ground coriander
½ tsp ground cumin
2 Tbsp lemon or lime juice
5 Tbsp oil

1. In a large mixing bowl, combine all the ingredients (reserving 2 Tbsp of the oil) and leave the beef and onions to marinate in the fridge for a minimum of 3 hours. Bring the marinated meat to room temperature before cooking.
2. Thread the beef and onions onto skewers.
3. Heat an outdoor grill to medium hot. When ready to cook, brush the grill grate with the reserved oil. This will prevent the meat from sticking.
4. Grill the skewers for 9–10 minutes, turning once every 3 minutes.

NOTE: If you are using bamboo skewers, soak the skewers in cold water for 15 minutes before threading and use celery stalks to cover the exposed parts of the skewers to prevent them from weakening and breaking during grilling.

Serves 4–6

GRILLED MEATBALLS IN PITA POCKETS WITH BEETROOT YOGHURT DIP

PITA BREADS
¾ cup cake flour or all-purpose white flour
½ tsp instant dry yeast
¼ tsp salt
pinch of brown or white sugar
1¼ tsp oil
¼ cup water

MEATBALLS
400 g beef mince
1 Tbsp garlic paste
½ Tbsp ginger paste
1 red onion, grated
¼ tsp salt
1½ Tbsp fresh breadcrumbs
1 tsp ground cumin
½ tsp ground coriander
½ cup finely chopped fresh coriander
1 tsp finely chopped fresh green chilli or ½ tsp red chilli powder
2 Tbsp oil

BEETROOT YOGHURT DIP
500 g creamy plain natural yoghurt or Greek yoghurt
3 Tbsp finely grated beetroot
1 tsp lemon or lime juice
¼ tsp salt

1. First make the pita breads. Combine the flour, yeast, salt, sugar and oil in a large mixing bowl. Add the water and knead the dough for 5 minutes or until well combined, smooth and stretchy. If needed, you can gradually add more water until the dough is stretchy.
2. Cover the mixing bowl with cling film or a damp tea towel and leave the dough to rise for 45 minutes.
3. Preheat the oven to 180 °C and line a baking tray with baking paper.
4. Transfer the risen dough to a floured work surface. Divide the dough into 4 equal balls and flatten them with your hands. Using a rolling pin, roll the balls of dough into circles 15 cm in diameter. Use your hands to gently turn the dough as you roll, sprinkling over a little flour each time you turn to prevent the dough from sticking to the rolling pin or work surface.
5. Arrange the dough circles on the lined baking tray, leaving about 5 cm between each. Bake for 20 minutes.
6. To make the meatballs, place the mince in a bowl and combine with the garlic paste, ginger paste, onion, salt, breadcrumbs, cumin, ground coriander, chopped fresh coriander and fresh chilli or chilli powder. Using your hands, shape the mince into small, elongated balls.
7. Heat an outdoor grill to medium hot. Brush the grill grate with the oil to prevent the meat from sticking. Place the meatballs 10 cm apart so that they are easier to turn while grilling. Grill for 4 minutes on each side.
8. To make the beetroot yoghurt dip, mix all the ingredients in a small bowl.
9. To serve, cut the baked pitas in half lengthwise to make pockets. Stuff the pita pockets with meatballs and drizzle over the dip or serve it on the side.

NOTE: You can also pan-fry the meatballs. Heat oil in a deep frying pan over medium to high heat and gently add the meatballs, spacing them evenly to make it easier to turn them during cooking. Fry for approximately 3 minutes on each side.

Serves 4

Grilled meatballs in pita pockets with beetroot yoghurt dip

Coconut milk is used in the preparation of at least half of all coastal East African dishes. Coconut rice is found in most coastal towns in the region, such as Tanga, Zanzibar and Pemba in Tanzania, and Mombasa, Lamu and Malindi in Kenya. My family enjoys the combination of barbecued beef served with coconut rice.

BEEF SKEWERS WITH YELLOW COCONUT RICE

400 g beef rump or fillet, cut into cubes
¼ each green and red bell peppers, deseeded and
    chopped into cubes
½ tsp salt
2 tsp ground black pepper
2 tsp garlic paste
2 dried bay leaves, finely crushed
1 tsp ground cumin
4 tsp Worcestershire sauce
oil for basting

YELLOW COCONUT RICE
1 cup long-grain rice, rinsed
1 tsp oil
¾ tsp cumin seeds
¼ cup fresh or tinned coconut cream
¼ tsp ground turmeric
¼ tsp salt
fresh coriander for garnishing

1. Place the beef and bell pepper cubes in a large mixing bowl and add the salt, black pepper, garlic paste, bay leaves, cumin and Worcestershire sauce. Toss the meat and peppers and leave to marinate for 30 minutes.
2. Thread the beef and bell pepper onto skewers.
3. Heat an outdoor grill to very hot and grill the skewers for 10–12 minutes, turning once every 2 minutes until cooked to your preference. Baste the skewers with oil each time you turn them.
4. To make the coconut rice, boil the rice in salted water according to the packet instructions until tender (avoid overcooking). Drain any remaining water and set aside the rice in a bowl to cool.
5. In a saucepan, heat the oil over medium to high heat and add the cumin seeds. Allow them to crackle for 15 seconds and then lower the heat. Add the coconut cream, turmeric and salt. Stir continuously for approximately 30 seconds.
6. Add the cooked rice and give it a gentle stir. Cover the saucepan with a lid and cook for approximately 4 minutes over low heat or until the rice has absorbed all the coconut cream and appears dry.
7. Garnish the rice with fresh coriander and serve with the beef skewers.

NOTE: If using a gas barbecue, heat to 400 °C. If using charcoal, ensure you have a well-lit bed of coals before cooking the meat.

Serves 4

Known as potato cutlets in Kenya and katlesi in Tanzania, these delicious mince-stuffed potato delicacies are enjoyed during the month of Ramadan, and make great appetisers as well as a main.

KATLESI [SPICY MINCE AND POTATO PATTIES]

250 g beef mince (you can also use chicken or mutton mince)
1 tsp garlic paste
½ tsp ginger paste
½ tsp salt
2 tsp chopped fresh green chilli or ½ tsp red chilli powder
¼ tsp garam masala

¼ tsp ground cumin
¼ tsp ground black pepper
1 tsp lemon or lime juice
¼ cup water
1 red onion, finely chopped
¼ cup chopped fresh coriander
3 small fresh mint leaves, chopped
2 cups oil for frying

COATING
5 large potatoes
1 cup fresh breadcrumbs
2 eggs
¼ tsp salt
¼ tsp red chilli powder
1 Tbsp chopped fresh coriander

1. In a large saucepan, combine the beef mince, garlic paste, ginger paste, salt, fresh chilli or chilli powder, garam masala, cumin, black pepper, lemon or lime juice and water. Boil over medium heat for 10 minutes, stirring every 2 minutes. Allow all the water to evaporate.

2. Remove from the heat and immediately add the onion, fresh coriander and mint. Stir well and let the mixture cool to room temperature. The mince should be dry and cool before using.

3. In the meantime, wash the potatoes and boil them in their skins in a saucepan of salted water for approximately 20 minutes until soft. Pierce them with a skewer or knife to test whether they are cooked.

4. Drain all the water and let the potatoes cool down until they are easy to handle. Peel off their skins and mash the potatoes until semi smooth.

5. Flatten a handful of potato mash and spoon some mince in the centre. Fold the mash over to seal in the mixture and roll into a smooth ball. Gently flatten the ball to resemble a bun or dinner roll. (Rub some oil on your palms and fingers to help with the rolling.) Make sure the potato patties are properly sealed with no cracks or transparent patches, as these may crack open while frying.

6. Prepare two dipping bowls. Place the breadcrumbs in the first bowl. In the second bowl, beat the eggs, salt, chilli powder and coriander with a fork.

7. First roll the sealed mince and potato patties in the breadcrumbs to evenly coat and then dip them in the egg mixture.

8. Heat the oil in a deep frying pan over medium heat and cook the patties for 30 seconds on each side or until they appear golden brown.

9. Serve with a dipping sauce of your choice.

Serves 4

CRUMBED BEEF ESCALOPES

400 g beef fillet
1 tsp garlic paste
½ Tbsp lemon or lime juice
1 tsp oil
¼ tsp ground black pepper
salt to taste
2 eggs, beaten
3 Tbsp fresh breadcrumbs
½ cup oil for frying

1. Thinly slice the beef and then lightly pound the slices between two sheets of cling film using a mallet, or flatten with a rolling pin.
2. Place the pounded beef escalopes in a bowl with the garlic paste, lemon or lime juice, oil, black pepper and salt to taste. Leave to marinate for 30 minutes.
3. Prepare two wide dipping bowls. Place the beaten eggs in the first bowl and season with salt and black pepper. Place the breadcrumbs in the second bowl.
4. Dip the marinated beef escalopes in the beaten egg first and then evenly coat with a thin layer of breadcrumbs.
5. Heat the oil in a frying pan over medium heat and shallow-fry the crumbed beef for 2 minutes on each side until golden brown.
6. Drain on paper towel before serving with a side of lemon wedges and French fries or salad.

Serves 4

BEEF BURGERS

BUNS
1¼ cups cake flour or all-purpose white flour
2 Tbsp oil
2 tsp instant dry yeast
½ tsp brown or white sugar
½ tsp salt
¼ cup warm full-cream milk mixed with ¼ cup warm water
1 egg
1 egg white (optional)
1 tsp sesame seeds (optional)

PATTIES
250 g lean beef mince
1 Tbsp oil
½ red onion, grated and liquid squeezed out
½ tsp garlic paste
¼ tsp ginger paste
¼ tsp ground black pepper
¼ tsp green chilli paste or red chilli powder (optional)
1 Tbsp finely chopped fresh coriander (optional)
salt to taste
1 egg

TO SERVE
butter
lettuce leaves
mayonnaise or sauce of your choice
thinly sliced tomato
thinly sliced onion rings
salt and ground black pepper

1. First make the burger buns. Mix all the ingredients, except the optional egg white and sesame seeds, in a bowl. Knead into a smooth dough using your hands, then cover the bowl with a damp tea towel and leave to rise for 45 minutes.
2. Preheat the oven to 180 °C and grease a baking tray.
3. Roll the risen dough into 4 balls the size of your palm and place them on the greased tray. You can brush the tops with egg white and sprinkle with sesame seeds, but this is optional.
4. Bake for 18–20 minutes. Let the buns rest for 5 minutes before transferring them to a plate.
5. To make the patties, combine all the ingredients in a large mixing bowl and refrigerate for approximately 30 minutes.
6. Roll the mince mixture into 4 balls and flatten into patties about 1 cm larger than your burger buns (the patties will shrink when cooked).
7. Place a frying pan over medium to high heat and use a brush to coat the bottom with oil. Cook the patties for 3 minutes on each side. Depending on the size of your frying pan, cook only a few patties at a time, leaving enough space between them to allow browning.
8. Cut the buns in half and butter lightly. Place lettuce on the bottom half, followed by some mayonnaise or sauce of your choice, a beef patty, tomato slices and raw onion rings. Season with salt and black pepper and cover with the top half of the bun. Use a toothpick or cocktail skewer to hold the burger in place, making handling easier.

Serves 4

Beef burgers

In different parts of the world, the word 'kebab' has different meanings. While in Europe it may refer to what Arabs call shawarma, in South Africa and parts of North America it means chunks of meat cooked on a skewer. In Asia and the Middle East, however, where this method of preparation supposedly originated, kebab refers to minced meat that is formed either around a skewer or into oblong or round meatballs, which are then grilled or pan-fried. Since East African cuisine is heavily influenced by Arab and Asian methods of cooking, this is the definition used in this part of the world. This deep-fried version is a hit across all East African countries. Fifty-year-old teashops from Dar es Salaam and Tanga to Mombasa serve them with cups of hot tea. An absolute must-try while in East Africa, kababu are a true foodie delight.

KABABU ZA KEEMA [DEEP-FRIED MEATBALLS]

300 g beef mince
1 red onion, finely chopped
¼ cup chopped fresh coriander
2 tsp garlic paste
1 tsp ginger paste
½ tsp salt
¼ tsp garam masala

½ tsp green chilli paste or 2 fresh green chillies,
    finely chopped
½ tsp curry powder
½ tsp ground cumin
1 egg
¼ cup fresh breadcrumbs
2 cups oil

1. Wash the beef mince and place in a strainer to drain any excess water.
2. In a mixing bowl, using a spatula, combine all the ingredients, except the oil. Roll the mixture into smooth 7.5 cm balls using the palms of your hands.
3. In a small saucepan, heat the oil over medium to high heat and gently deep-fry the meatballs until they appear dark brown.
4. Thread onto skewers or leave as is and serve with coconut chutney or a mint and coriander dip.

Serves 2–4

Having mastered the art of cooking different types of lamb dishes in Kenya, I find these shanks the easiest to make on a busy weeknight, as they require minimal preparation.

ROASTED LAMB SHANKS

2 x 400–450 g lamb shanks
1 tsp coarsely ground black pepper
½ tsp salt
2 tsp apple cider vinegar
2 tsp lemon or lime juice
2 tsp oil
10 garlic cloves
2 carrots, peeled and halved

2 red onions, halved
1 green apple, peeled and quartered
handful of fresh rosemary stems and leaves
    (you can also use dried rosemary)

1. In a large bowl, marinate the lamb shanks in the black pepper, salt, apple cider vinegar, lemon or lime juice and oil for a minimum of 1 hour.
2. Preheat the oven to 220 °C.
3. Place the garlic cloves, carrots, onions and apple in the centre of a deep ovenproof dish or baking tray.
4. Place the marinated shanks on top and cover them with rosemary.
5. Cover the dish or baking tray with aluminium foil, sealing well to ensure there are no gaps for heat to escape during cooking.
6. Roast for 2 hours, turning the shanks only once after the first hour.
7. Once cooked, place the shanks on a serving dish. Strain the liquid from the roasting dish or tray and use a spoon to drizzle it over the lamb. Serve any remaining cooking juices on the side if desired.

Serves 2 |

LAMB BIRIYANI

500 g stewing lamb
7 cups water
oil
3 red onions, thinly sliced
1 cinnamon stick
3 whole cloves
3 cardamom pods
6 medium tomatoes, grated
2 Tbsp tomato purée or paste
½ tsp salt
2 tsp garam masala
½ tsp red chilli powder

½ cup chopped fresh coriander
1½ cups wholegrain or basmati
   rice, rinsed
2 tsp cumin seeds
5 drops yellow food colouring
5 drops orange food colouring
2 Tbsp melted ghee or salted butter

MARINADE
2 Tbsp lemon or lime juice
1 Tbsp garlic paste
½ Tbsp ginger paste

2 Tbsp chopped fresh mint
   (reserve ½ tsp for garnishing)
1 Tbsp Greek yoghurt
½ tsp ground cinnamon
½ tsp ground black pepper
¼ tsp ground cardamom
½ tsp ground cumin
½ tsp ground coriander
¼ tsp ground turmeric
1 tsp salt

1. Combine all the marinade ingredients in a large bowl. Add the lamb and marinate for 30 minutes at room temperature. Place the marinated lamb in a large saucepan, add the water and bring to the boil over high heat. Boil for 40 minutes or until the lamb is tender. Once cooked, strain the lamb and reserve the stock.

2. In a frying pan, heat 1 cup oil over high heat and fry the onions until they appear brown and crisp. Remove from the heat and set aside on paper towel.

3. In a large saucepan, heat 2 Tbsp oil over medium heat and add the cinnamon stick, whole cloves and cardamom pods. Temper (toast) for 15 seconds and then add the rest of the ingredients in the following order: grated tomatoes, tomato purée or paste, half the fried onions, salt, garam masala, red chilli powder and half the chopped fresh coriander. Stir, cover the pan with a lid and simmer for 8–10 minutes until thickened.

4. Add the lamb together with 1 cup of the reserved stock and cook, covered, for a further 10 minutes. Remove from the heat.

5. Boil the rice in salted water according to the packet instructions, making sure it does not stick to the bottom of the saucepan. If the rice is cooked and there is water remaining, strain and return the rice to the saucepan.

6. In a separate small saucepan, heat 1 Tbsp oil over low heat and temper the cumin seeds for 20–30 seconds. Add the cumin seeds to the cooked rice along with the yellow and orange food colourings. Mix well with a spatula and set side.

7. Preheat the oven to 180 °C. Grease the bottom and sides of an ovenproof dish with oil.

8. Using a spatula, spread half the rice over the bottom of the greased dish, ensuring the base is fully covered. Pour over the lamb gravy to cover the rice. Spread the rest of the rice over the lamb gravy layer.

9. Sprinkle over the remaining fried onions and fresh coriander, as well as the reserved fresh mint.

10. Pour the melted ghee or butter over the top and cover the dish with aluminium foil. Bake for 20 minutes.

NOTE: Serve with fresh papadums and raita: in a bowl, combine 2 cups plain natural yoghurt, 1 chopped tomato, 1 chopped onion, ¼ tsp ground cumin, ¼ tsp red chilli powder (optional) and salt to taste.

Serves 4

Lamb biriyani

Kenya in particular is known for its delicious lamb dishes. Several restaurants and cafés will have nyama choma on their menu, which means barbecued or roasted meat. This recipe includes interesting additions such as mint and pomegranate seeds that add an abundance of flavour.

NYAMA CHOMA [BARBECUED LAMB]

1 kg lamb chops
oil for basting
fresh mint leaves for garnishing
2 Tbsp pomegranate seeds
    (optional)

MARINADE
2 tsp garlic paste
1 tsp ginger paste

½ tsp ground coriander
½ tsp ground cumin
½ tsp curry powder
¼ garam masala
½ tsp tandoori masala (optional)
¼ tsp red chilli powder
¼ tsp coarsely ground
    black pepper
2 Tbsp lemon or lime juice

1 Tbsp tomato purée or paste
½ Tbsp Greek yoghurt
½ tsp bicarbonate of soda
    (optional)
2 tsp chopped fresh coriander
2 tsp oil

1. Place the lamb chops in a large mixing bowl and add all the marinade ingredients. Mix well, cover the bowl with cling film and leave to marinate in the fridge for 3 hours.
2. Heat an outdoor grill to very hot and grill the lamb chops, basting with oil and turning frequently until cooked, approximately 10 minutes (cooking time will vary with the thickness of the chops).
3. Garnish with the fresh mint leaves and pomegranate seeds (if using).

NOTES: If using a gas barbecue, heat to 400 °C. If using charcoal, create an even charcoal bed and ensure that most of the coals are well lit before cooking the meat. The distance between the meat on the grill and the coals should not be more than 10 cm.
Tandoori masala is an Indian spice mix consisting of cumin, coriander, cloves, cinnamon, ginger, garlic, chilli, turmeric, mace and salt.

Serves 2–4 |

Whole roast spring chicken with vegetables

Poultry

This is my favourite last-minute meal. It does not require any additional marinating time and overall preparation time is minimal. And it is deliciously healthy.

WHOLE ROAST SPRING CHICKEN WITH VEGETABLES

1 spring chicken or poussin, skinned
2 red or white onions
1 tsp garlic paste
½ tsp ginger paste
¼ tsp salt
2 tsp lemon or lime juice
1 Tbsp oil

5 large garlic cloves
1 jalapeño chilli pepper or any fresh chilli
    of your choice, chopped
1 carrot, peeled and halved lengthwise,
    or 4–6 whole baby carrots
2 potatoes, peeled and halved
1 Tbsp salted butter

1. Preheat the oven to 190 °C and grease a large ovenproof dish or baking tray.
2. Pat the chicken dry with paper towel.
3. Quarter one of the onions and set aside. Grate the other onion and use your hands to squeeze out all the liquid. Reserve this liquid and discard the grated onion.
4. Mix the garlic paste, ginger paste, salt, lemon or lime juice, oil and onion liquid. Rub this mixture all over the chicken and stuff the cavity with the garlic cloves and chopped chilli.
5. Tie the legs with kitchen twine or secure with a skewer: place the chicken breast-side up, hold the legs together with one hand and use the other hand to insert a skewer below the knee joint and push it through the legs.
6. Place the chicken, breast-side down, in the centre of the greased dish or tray and surround with the quartered onion, carrots and potatoes.
7. Bake for 30 minutes, then turn the chicken, brush the top with the butter and cook for a further 35 minutes.
8. Transfer the chicken and roasted vegetables to a serving dish and drizzle over 2 Tbsp of the roasting juices.

Serves 2

Stir-fries make great appetisers and are common on East African menus, served in hilltop cafés and restaurants, as well as safari lodges. My version of stir-fry includes locally harvested mangoes and cashew nuts. Tanzania is the largest exporter of cashew nuts in Africa. Locally farmed cashews tossed in salads and stir-fries add a welcome crunch.

STIR-FRIED CHICKEN WITH A TRIO OF BELL PEPPERS AND MANGO

4 deboned chicken breasts
1 red bell pepper
1 green bell pepper
1 yellow bell pepper
1 Tbsp garlic paste
1 tsp honey
3 Tbsp soy sauce
½ tsp salt
2 Tbsp oil
3 garlic cloves, chopped
2 Tbsp finely julienned ginger
1 cup shredded cabbage

1 spring onion, white part sliced diagonally
 and leaves chopped
1 carrot, peeled and julienned
1 tsp oyster sauce (optional)
¼ tsp coarsely ground black pepper
1 tsp dried red chilli flakes
1 ripe mango, peeled and cut lengthwise into strips
handful of roasted cashew nuts (optional)

1. Slice the chicken breasts lengthwise into strips 7.5 cm long and 2.5 cm wide.
2. Halve, deseed and slice the 3 bell peppers lengthwise into strips 1 cm wide.
3. In a mixing bowl, combine the chicken strips with the garlic paste, honey, 1 Tbsp soy sauce and ¼ tsp salt. Leave to marinate at room temperature for 30 minutes.
4. In a wok or deep frying pan, heat half the oil over high heat and cook the chicken strips for approximately 3 minutes, tossing frequently until cooked. Transfer the chicken to a bowl and set aside.
5. In the same wok or pan, heat the remaining oil and sauté the chopped garlic and ginger for approximately 15 seconds or until just fragrant, ensuring the garlic does not brown.
6. Add the bell pepper strips, cabbage, white part of the spring onion and carrot. Toss well.
7. Add the remaining soy sauce and salt along with the oyster sauce (if using) and black pepper. Sprinkle over the chopped spring onion leaves and toss well. Sauté for approximately 1 minute over medium to high heat.
8. Add the cooked chicken strips and chilli flakes, give it a good final toss and remove from the heat. Stir in the mango strips and roasted cashew nuts (if using). Serve immediately.

Serves 4

PAN-FRIED CHICKEN BREASTS WITH TOMATO AND CORIANDER SALSA

4 deboned chicken breasts
2 tsp garlic paste
¼ tsp cayenne pepper
½ tsp ground coriander
1 tsp ground cumin
¼ tsp salt
2 Tbsp butter
fresh coriander for garnishing

TOMATO AND CORIANDER SALSA

1 Tbsp oil
1 red onion, chopped
4 ripe tomatoes, chopped, or 400 g cherry
    tomatoes, quartered
2 fresh green chillies, chopped, or ¼ tsp green
    chilli paste
salt to taste
3 Tbsp chopped fresh coriander or 1 Tbsp ground

1. Marinate the chicken breasts in the garlic paste, cayenne pepper, coriander, cumin and salt for a minimum of 30 minutes.

2. To make the tomato and coriander salsa, heat the oil in a saucepan over medium to high heat. Add the onion, tomatoes, chillies or chilli paste and salt. Sauté for approximately 3 minutes, stirring frequently. Add the fresh or ground coriander, stir and simmer for 1 minute. Set aside.

3. In a frying pan, melt the butter over medium heat and fry the marinated chicken breasts on each side until firm to the touch and cooked through.

4. Spoon the tomato and coriander salsa over the cooked chicken, garnish with fresh coriander and serve.

Serves 2

In East Africa, 'kebab' refers to minced meat that is formed either around a skewer or into oblong meatballs, which are then grilled or pan-fried. In this recipe, the kebabs are made without a skewer and are pan-fried in minimal oil. I find this to be the most efficient method of making delicious kebabs!

PAN-FRIED CHICKEN KEBABS WITH MINT YOGHURT DIP

400 g chicken mince
1 red or white onion, chopped
2 tsp garlic paste
1 tsp ginger paste
2 fresh green chillies, finely chopped, or
    ¼ tsp green chilli paste
½ tsp ground black pepper
½ tsp salt
1 tsp ground coriander
1 tsp ground cumin
¼ tsp garam masala
½ Tbsp Greek yoghurt

¼ cup chopped fresh parsley
1 egg
1 Tbsp butter

MINT YOGHURT DIP
¼ cup Greek yoghurt
¼ tsp garlic paste
salt to taste
1 tsp chopped fresh mint
fresh mint leaves and pomegranate seeds for
    garnishing (optional)

1. To make the mint yoghurt dip, combine the yoghurt, garlic paste, salt and chopped mint in a small bowl. Garnish with the mint leaves and pomegranate seeds (if using). Refrigerate until ready to use.
2. To make the kebabs, place all the ingredients, except the butter, in a mixing bowl. Mix well using a spatula and then roll or pat into oblong-shaped balls, 12–15 cm long.
3. Melt the butter in a frying pan over medium heat and pan-fry the chicken kebabs for 7–8 minutes, turning every minute, until cooked through.
4. Serve with the mint yoghurt dip.

Serves 4

Chicken tikka originated in India, was brought to East Africa by generations of Indian immigrants, and adapted by incorporating local spices such as turmeric, chilli powder, cumin, cloves, cardamom and cinnamon. Tandoori masala is readily available. It is a combination of spices that gets its vibrant colour from red chilli powder and ground turmeric.

GRILLED CHICKEN TIKKA
WITH ONION AND GREEN BELL PEPPER

500 g deboned chicken breasts
1 large green bell pepper, deseeded and cut into
    5 cm squares
1 large red onion, cut into 5 cm squares
¼ cup oil
1 Tbsp garlic paste
½ Tbsp ginger paste
¼ tsp ground turmeric

½ tsp red chilli powder or cayenne pepper
2 Tbsp tandoori masala
2 tsp ground cumin
1 tsp ground coriander
1 tsp garam masala
2 Tbsp lemon or lime juice
2 Tbsp Greek yoghurt
1 Tbsp tomato purée or paste

1. Pat the chicken breasts dry with paper towel and cut into 5 cm cubes.
2. Place the chicken, bell pepper and onion in a mixing bowl with 2 Tbsp of the oil. Add the rest of the ingredients, gently mix to coat and then leave to marinate in the fridge for a minimum of 2 hours. Bring the marinated chicken to room temperature before cooking.
3. Thread the chicken, bell pepper and onion onto skewers.
4. Heat an outdoor grill to medium hot. Brush the grill grate with some of the remaining oil. This will prevent the chicken from sticking.
5. Grill the skewers for 13–15 minutes, turning every 3 minutes and brushing the exposed side with oil.
6. Serve with a side salad or French fries.

Serves 2

Spaghetti is surprisingly popular in Tanzania, and is prepared in many different ways. My favourite version includes cooking cream and milk, which give it a rich and creamy texture.

CHICKEN SPAGHETTI IN A CREAMY GARLIC SAUCE

250 g spaghetti
1 Tbsp butter
1 tsp crushed garlic
¾ cup chicken stock (made with ¼ stock cube or
    ¼ Tbsp stock powder)
1 Tbsp cake flour or all-purpose white flour
¾ cup cooking cream (such as Nestlé Dessert &
    Cooking Cream)
¾ cup full-cream milk
1 tsp dried origanum, plus extra for garnishing
1 tsp dried red chilli flakes, plus extra for garnishing

¼ tsp salt
2 tsp oil
1 small red or white onion, finely chopped
2 deboned chicken breasts, sliced lengthwise into
    5 cm thick pieces

1. Bring a saucepan of salted water to the boil and cook the spaghetti for approximately 9 minutes or until al dente. Drain and set aside.
2. In a separate large saucepan, melt the butter over medium to high heat and sauté the garlic until fragrant, ensuring it does not brown.
3. Using a whisk, stir in the chicken stock, then add half of the flour and whisk well. Stir in the cooking cream, followed by the milk and the remaining flour. Whisk well to ensure there are no lumps.
4. Stir in the origanum, chilli flakes and salt, and simmer for 3–4 minutes until the sauce is thick enough to coat the back of a spoon. Remove from the heat.
5. In a deep frying pan or saucepan, heat the oil over medium to high heat and sauté the onion until translucent.
6. Add the chicken and sauté, tossing frequently, until cooked through.
7. Lower the heat and add the creamy garlic sauce. Combine well and then mix in the cooked spaghetti. Garnish with extra origanum and red chilli flakes.

Serves 4

Frankie rolls are chapattis stuffed with meat and vegetables, and seasoned with a combination of spices to give them bags of flavour.

CHICKEN FRANKIE ROLL

2 Tbsp oil
2 eggs, beaten
1 tsp garlic paste
½ tsp ginger paste
3 tomatoes, grated or blended
1 Tbsp tomato sauce
1 tsp ground cumin
1 tsp ground coriander
1 tsp curry powder
½ tsp red chilli powder
¼ tsp salt

200 g deboned chicken breasts, cubed
1 tsp lemon or lime juice
¼ red onion, sliced into half moons
chopped fresh coriander for garnishing

CHAPATTI DOUGH
1 cup cake flour or all-purpose white flour or
    whole-wheat flour
¼ tsp salt
1 Tbsp oil
¼ cup water

1. First make the chapatti dough. In a bowl, mix the flour, salt and oil. Knead into a dough by adding the water at intervals, until it feels smooth to the touch and can be easily rolled on a flat surface.
2. Dust your work surface with some flour and, using a rolling pin, roll the dough into a circle 23 cm in diameter.
3. Place a frying pan over medium heat. Lay the chapatti in the heated pan for 5–10 seconds or until it just begins to bubble, then turn over and cook the other side until it too bubbles. Lower the heat. Flip over again and use a spatula to smear some oil from the centre to the edges of the chapatti. Flip it again and smear the other side. Remove from the heat.
4. Heat half of the oil in a clean 15 cm frying pan over medium heat and pour in the beaten eggs. Tilt the pan to make a very thin omelette and cook each side for 15–20 seconds (do not overcook the egg). Transfer to a plate and set aside.
5. Heat the remaining oil in a saucepan over medium heat. Add the garlic paste and ginger paste and sauté for 30 seconds or until just fragrant. Add the tomatoes, tomato sauce, cumin, coriander, curry powder, chilli powder and salt. Stir well and simmer for 2 minutes.
6. Add the chicken and cover the saucepan with a lid. Cook for approximately 5 minutes over low heat, ensuring the mixture does not cook dry. Add the lemon or lime juice just before turning off the heat, then give it a good stir.
7. Place the chapatti on your work surface and position the omelette on top. Arrange the sliced onion in a line along the centre, leaving at least 2 cm from each edge to avoid spillage. Spoon the chicken on top of the onion, sprinkle over some chopped fresh coriander and roll up the chapatti. Slice in half and wrap the bottom half of each roll with baking paper for easy handling while you eat.

NOTE: To save time, use a readymade store-bought tortilla.

Serves 2

Chicken frankie roll

STUFFED CHICKEN with a CREAMY TOMATO SAUCE

4 deboned chicken breasts
2 tsp garlic paste
½ Tbsp ginger paste
½ tsp dried origanum
¼ tsp salt
¼ cup chopped green bell pepper
¼ cup grated mozzarella cheese
3 Tbsp olive oil
fresh rocket and baby spinach for garnishing

CREAMY TOMATO SAUCE

1 Tbsp butter
3 garlic cloves, chopped
¼ cup chopped celery
4 cups chopped tomatoes (you can use tinned chopped tomatoes)
¼ tsp salt
¼ tsp ground black pepper
1 tsp dried red chilli flakes
½ tsp dried origanum
¼ cup cooking cream (such as Nestlé Dessert & Cooking Cream)

1. To make the creamy tomato sauce, melt the butter in a large saucepan over medium heat and sauté the garlic for 15 seconds, making sure it does not brown.
2. Add the celery and sauté until soft.
3. Add the tomatoes, salt, black pepper, red chilli flakes and origanum. Cover the saucepan with a lid and simmer for 4–5 minutes. Remove from the heat and allow to cool to room temperature.
4. Pour the cooled tomato mixture into a blender and blend on low speed for 20 seconds or until smooth. Return the mixture to the saucepan, stir in the cream and simmer for 1 minute. Set aside.
5. Place the whole chicken breasts in a mixing bowl and add the garlic paste, ginger paste, origanum and salt. Rub the mixture into the chicken breasts to ensure they are well coated.
6. Place the chicken breasts on a chopping board. Insert a knife in the side of the thickest part of each breast and make a slit 3–4 cm long (depending on the size of the chicken breast), making sure that the slit runs only three-quarters of the way through.
7. Stuff the chicken breasts with the bell pepper and cheese. Gently press the breasts to close them to avoid the stuffing spilling out. You can use skewers to keep them closed, if necessary.
8. Heat the oil in a frying pan over medium heat and cook the stuffed chicken breasts for approximately 3 minutes on each side or until the chicken is cooked through. For larger chicken breasts, you may need to increase cooking time to 5–6 minutes per side.
9. Coat the chicken breasts in the creamy tomato sauce and serve, garnished with fresh rocket. Any leftover sauce could be served on the side.

Serves 4

Get that smoky-flavoured butter chicken right in your own kitchen! I've brought an authentic African twist to the world-famous chicken tikka masala by adding a live coal to the infusion process. The smoked flavour in this delicacy cannot be created using any other method. Serve piping hot with chapattis.

SMOKED BUTTER CHICKEN

500 g deboned chicken breasts, cut into 5 cm cubes
1 Tbsp garlic paste
1 Tbsp ginger paste
½ cup Greek yoghurt
½ tsp red chilli powder
½ tsp salt
1 Tbsp oil
½ cup cashew nuts

½ cup whole almonds
3 Tbsp butter
3 large tomatoes, blended
¼ tsp garam masala
1 tsp ground cumin
1 Tbsp tomato sauce
1 Tbsp kasuri methi (see note below)

1. Place the chicken in a medium heatproof bowl and add the garlic paste, ginger paste, yoghurt, red chilli powder and half of the salt. Toss to coat.
2. Place a small ramekin in the centre of the bowl and arrange the marinated chicken around it.
3. Heat a piece of charcoal on direct heat for 10 minutes (you can do this on either a gas or electric stove, taking as long as necessary to light the coal so that it's properly on fire). Using tongs, carefully place the live coal in the ramekin.
4. Pour the oil on the coal and immediately cover the whole bowl with aluminium foil or a lid. Leave the chicken to smoke at room temperature for a minimum of 45 minutes.
5. Chop the cashew nuts and almonds and grind them into a smooth powder in a spice or coffee grinder.
6. In a large saucepan, melt 2 Tbsp of the butter over medium heat and add the smoked chicken. Stir well to coat and ensure the chicken does not stick to the bottom of the pan.
7. Add the rest of the ingredients, including the ground nuts and the remaining salt. Cook for 10 minutes, stirring frequently.
8. Melt the remaining butter and pour over the bubbling hot chicken just before serving.

NOTE: Kasuri methi, or dried fenugreek leaves, is available at some specialist supermarkets. You can substitute with fenugreek seeds or a pinch of fenugreek powder.

Serves 4 |

CREAMY CHICKEN-STUFFED AVOCADOS WITH ONION AND TOMATO SALSA

1 deboned chicken breast, chopped into 2.5 cm cubes
½ tsp garlic paste
½ tsp finely chopped fresh green chilli or red chilli powder
1 tsp honey
½ tsp Worcestershire sauce
¼ tsp salt
1 tsp ground cumin
½ tsp ground coriander
½ tsp lemon or lime juice
1 Tbsp olive oil
2 garlic cloves, chopped

½ cup cooking cream (such as Nestlé Dessert & Cooking Cream)
¼ cup grated Cheddar cheese
2 avocados, halved
2 Tbsp chopped fresh coriander

ONION AND TOMATO SALSA
½ red onion, chopped
1 tomato, chopped
1 tsp lemon or lime juice
3 garlic cloves, chopped
salt to taste

1. Place the chicken in a bowl and add the garlic paste, fresh chilli or chilli powder, honey, Worcestershire sauce, salt, cumin, coriander and lemon or lime juice. Toss to coat.
2. Heat the oil in a saucepan over medium to high heat and sauté the chopped garlic until just fragrant (avoid browning). Add the marinated chicken and sauté until cooked.
3. Lower the heat and add the cream. Simmer for approximately 1 minute, then stir in the cheese and simmer for another minute. Remove from the heat and allow to cool.
4. To make the salsa, combine all the ingredients in a small bowl and mix well.
5. Stuff each avocado half first with a spoonful of creamy chicken and then a spoonful of salsa. Garnish with the chopped fresh coriander.

Serves 4

Creamy chicken-stuffed avocados with onion and tomato salsa

CHICKEN ESCALOPES

4 deboned chicken breasts
1 tsp ground cumin
2 tsp garlic paste
1 tsp ginger paste
1 Tbsp lemon or lime juice
¼ tsp salt
½ tsp green chilli paste or 2 tsp finely chopped fresh
   green chilli or ¼ tsp cayenne pepper

2 Tbsp cake flour or all-purpose white flour, seasoned
   with a pinch each of ground black pepper, ground
   cumin and salt
2 eggs, beaten
1 cup fresh breadcrumbs
1½ cups oil

1. Place the chicken breasts on a flat surface, preferably a chopping board, and pat dry with paper towel. Place a sheet of cling film on top and gently pound or flatten the chicken using a mallet or rolling pin.
2. Place the flattened chicken breasts in a shallow bowl and rub with the cumin, garlic paste, ginger paste, lemon or lime juice, salt and chilli paste, fresh chilli or cayenne pepper.
3. Prepare three wide bowls: one for the seasoned flour, one for the beaten eggs and one for the breadcrumbs.
4. First coat the marinated chicken breasts in the flour, shaking off any excess flour before dipping them into the beaten egg to coat evenly. Finally, coat the egg-washed chicken breasts in the breadcrumbs.
5. Heat the oil in a wide frying pan over medium heat and shallow-fry the chicken escalopes for approximately 2 minutes on each side or until golden brown.

Serves 4

Chicken in Kiswahili is kuku and spinach is mchicha. Both are cooked daily in many homes across the region. This recipe makes for a perfect weekday meal.

KUKU WA KUCHOMA NA MCHICHA
[GRILLED CHICKEN THIGHS WITH A CREAMY SPINACH SAUCE]

6 chicken thighs
2 tsp ground cumin
1 tsp ground coriander
1 tsp dried origanum
1 Tbsp garlic paste
½ tsp cayenne pepper
¼ tsp paprika
1 Tbsp lemon or lime juice
½ tsp salt
3 Tbsp oil

CREAMY SPINACH SAUCE
½ Tbsp butter
1 Tbsp chopped garlic
4 cups roughly chopped raw baby spinach
¾ cup cooking cream (such as Nestlé Dessert & Cooking Cream)
½ cup full-cream milk
¼ tsp salt
¼ tsp coarsely ground black pepper
½ cup grated Cheddar cheese
fresh basil for garnishing

1. Place the chicken thighs in a large mixing bowl with the cumin, coriander, origanum, garlic paste, cayenne pepper, paprika, lemon or lime juice and salt. Rub the ingredients into the chicken and leave to marinate for 30 minutes at room temperature or up to 24 hours in the fridge.

2. To make the spinach sauce, melt the butter in a small saucepan over medium heat and sauté the garlic and spinach for approximately 2 minutes. Add the cream, milk, salt and black pepper. Turn up the heat and simmer until the cream starts to bubble, stirring frequently. Take the saucepan off the heat and add the cheese, mixing until the cheese melts.

3. Heat an outdoor grill to medium hot and grease the grill grate with some of the oil. Place the marinated chicken thighs on the grill, skin-side down, and cook for 12–15 minutes. Flip over, baste with some more oil and grill for another 7–8 minutes. To check if the chicken is cooked, make a small incision in the thickest part of the thigh. If the meat is pink, grill for an additional 2–3 minutes.

4. Serve the spinach sauce with the chicken thighs, as you prefer, when ready to serve. Garnish with fresh basil.

NOTE: You can also roast the chicken. Preheat the oven to 200 °C. Brush a baking tray or ovenproof dish with oil and roast the chicken thighs, skin-side down, for approximately 25 minutes. Turn the thighs and roast for another 15 minutes.

Serves 2–4

Kenyan-style poussin sauce is a spicy, fiery sauce that has become popular all over East Africa. It can be served with French fries or used as a marinade for chicken, which is where its name originated. For those daring, spicy-food lovers, these Kenyan wings, invented by chilli fanatics who didn't give a hoot about being healthy, are magical. They are a hit in my house, and I swear my husband loves me a little more each time I make them.

FIERY POUSSIN CHICKEN WINGS

10 chicken wings
1 Tbsp garlic paste
½ Tbsp ginger paste
1 tsp red chilli powder
3 Tbsp lemon or lime juice
1 tsp salt
3 cups oil
chopped spring onion for garnishing (optional)

POUSSIN SAUCE
1 Tbsp oil
1 tsp garlic paste
2 Tbsp lemon or lime juice
1 tsp red chilli powder
¼ tsp paprika
pinch of salt

1. Place the chicken wings in a large mixing bowl with the garlic paste, ginger paste, red chilli powder, lemon or lime juice and salt. Mix well and leave to marinate for 30 minutes at room temperature.
2. In a deep frying pan or saucepan suitable for frying, heat the oil over high heat and deep-fry the marinated chicken wings for 5 minutes or until they appear crispy.
3. To make the sauce, heat the oil in a small saucepan over low heat. Add the garlic paste and immediately remove from the heat to ensure the garlic does not brown. Add the remaining ingredients and stir well. Pour over the hot chicken wings just before serving.
4. Garnish with chopped spring onion (if using).

Serves 4

CHICKEN AND VEGETABLE SPRING ROLLS

2 deboned chicken breasts, cut into 1 cm cubes
2 tsp garlic paste
1 tsp ginger paste
¾ tsp salt
4 cups oil
½ cup grated carrot

½ cup grated cabbage
1 Tbsp soy sauce
¼ tsp ground black pepper
¼ cup chopped spring onion leaves
1 cup cake flour or all-purpose white flour
¼ cup water at room temperature

1. Place the chicken, garlic paste, ginger paste and ¼ tsp of the salt in a bowl and mix well.
2. In a wok or deep frying pan, heat half the oil over medium to high heat and cook the marinated chicken for 1–2 minutes, tossing frequently to prevent the chicken from sticking to the bottom of the wok or pan.
3. Add the carrot, cabbage, soy sauce, black pepper and ¼ tsp of the salt. Toss for 30 seconds and then remove from the heat.
4. Add the spring onion leaves and mix well. Transfer to a bowl and allow to cool to room temperature.
5. In a separate clean bowl, mix the flour with the remaining ¼ tsp salt. Make a dough by adding the water at intervals until the dough is soft and easy to roll.
6. Dust your work surface with some flour and, using a rolling pin, roll the dough into a 20 x 20 cm square. Cut this into 4 smaller 10 cm squares.
7. Line a spoonful of the chicken filling on the bottom third of each square. Fold in the sides and brush all the edges with a paste made from 2 tsp flour and 1 tsp water. Roll up the spring roll, making sure all the sides are well sealed.
8. Heat the remaining oil in a deep frying pan over medium to high heat and deep-fry the spring rolls until they are golden brown.
9. Use a sharp knife to cut the spring rolls diagonally in half before serving with a side of sweet chilli sauce.

NOTES: To save time, you can use readymade store-bought spring-roll wrappers.
Smaller versions of the spring rolls make a great party snack.
Go vegetarian by simply omitting the chicken.

Serves 4

Fish masala curry

Seafood

FISH MASALA CURRY

2 x 200 g fish fillets (I prefer Nile perch, kingklip or tuna)
2 tsp lemon or lime juice
2 tsp garlic paste
salt
1 cup water
2 Tbsp oil
1 tsp cumin seeds
½ red onion, chopped

3 large tomatoes, grated or blended
1 Tbsp tomato purée or paste
½ tsp red chilli powder
¼ tsp ground cumin
¼ tsp ground turmeric
1 Tbsp curry powder
½ tsp garam masala
handful of chopped fresh coriander

1. Wash the fish fillets and pat dry with paper towel. Place in a wide bowl and gently rub with half of the lemon or lime juice, half of the garlic paste and salt to taste. Marinate at room temperature for 15 minutes.
2. Place the marinated fish in a saucepan with ¾ cup water and bring to the boil over medium heat. Boil for approximately 1 minute, then gently turn the fillets and boil for another minute. Drain and set aside.
3. In a separate large saucepan, heat the oil over high heat and add the cumin seeds. Let them crackle for approximately 15 seconds, then add the onion and sauté until it starts to brown. Add the remaining garlic paste and stir well.
4. Add the tomatoes, tomato purée or paste, red chilli powder, ground cumin, turmeric, curry powder, garam masala, ¼ tsp salt and the remaining ¼ cup water. Stir well, cover the saucepan with a lid and simmer for 10–12 minutes over medium heat.
5. Turn down the heat and gently place the boiled fish fillets flat in the simmering curry. Continue to simmer, partially covered, for 3–4 minutes.
6. Carefully flip the fillets and add the chopped fresh coriander. Simmer for another 2 minutes. The curry should be rich and thick.
7. Serve with chapattis, pita breads or steamed rice.

Serves 2

Fish is as popular as other meats in Tanzanian and Ugandan homes. Saltwater fish is consumed along Tanzania's eastern seaboard and in the southern region, but in the northwest and beyond to Uganda, freshwater fish is the preferred option due to the proximity of magnificent Lake Victoria. My favourite method of preparation involves organic basil from my herb patch at home and the sharp tang of celery, which ensures a tasty outcome, yet retains the delicate flavour of the lightly pan-fried fresh fish, regardless of what type of fish you use.

CELERY AND BASIL FISH

2 x 200 g fish fillets (I prefer Nile perch, kingklip or tuna)
¼ tsp salt
½ tsp ground black pepper
1 tsp green chilli paste
2 tsp lemon or lime juice

1 tsp cake flour or all-purpose white flour
2 Tbsp butter
½ cup chopped celery
2 Tbsp chopped fresh sweet basil, plus extra for garnishing
8 garlic cloves, chopped

1. Wash the fish fillets and pat dry with paper towel. Gently rub in the salt, black pepper, green chilli paste and lemon or lime juice.
2. Sprinkle both sides of the fish fillets with the flour and place them on a plate.
3. In a frying pan, melt the butter over medium to high heat and sauté the celery and basil until the celery has softened. Add the garlic and sauté for approximately 30 seconds.
4. Carefully place the fish in the pan and spoon over the sautéed celery, basil and garlic. Cook for 4 minutes, then turn the fish, spoon the sauce over the exposed side and cook for another 4 minutes.
5. Serve the fish smothered in the sautéed celery, basil and garlic and garnished with chopped sweet basil.

Serves 2

CHICKEN AND PRAWN FRIED RICE

1 cup long-grain rice
200 g small prawns, cleaned, peeled and deveined
¾ tsp garlic paste
100 g chicken mince
¼ tsp ginger paste
3 Tbsp cooking oil
2 eggs, beaten
2 Tbsp sesame oil
4 garlic cloves, chopped

½ cup grated cabbage
½ cup chopped green bell pepper
¼ cup chopped shallots
½ cup chopped carrot
3 Tbsp soy sauce
2 tsp red chilli paste or finely chopped fresh red chilli
½ tsp salt
¼ tsp ground black pepper
¼ cup chopped spring onion leaves

1. Bring a lightly salted saucepan of water to the boil. Add the rice and boil for approximately 15 minutes over medium heat until tender. Drain any excess water and set aside.
2. Marinate the prawns with ½ tsp of the garlic paste in one bowl, and combine the chicken mince with the rest of the garlic paste and the ginger paste in another bowl.
3. In a wok or large deep frying pan, heat 1 Tbsp of the cooking oil over medium heat and add the beaten eggs. Swirl and scramble the eggs until cooked. Set aside in a bowl.
4. In the same wok or pan, heat another 1 Tbsp of the cooking oil over medium to high heat and sauté the chicken mince for approximately 2 minutes. Set aside in a bowl.
5. Add the rest of the cooking oil to the wok or pan and sauté the prawns until they turn pink and opaque. Set aside in a bowl.
6. Continue to use the same wok or pan (by doing so, you will add more flavour to the rice). Heat the sesame oil over high heat and sauté the garlic for approximately 15 seconds, making sure not to brown it.
7. Add the cabbage, bell pepper, shallots and carrot to the wok. Toss to combine well and sauté for approximately 1 minute over high heat.
8. Add the cooked rice followed by the soy sauce, chilli paste or fresh chilli and ¼ tsp of the salt. Mix well.
9. Add the cooked prawns, cooked chicken mince and scrambled egg. Mix well, sprinkle over the black pepper and remaining salt, and toss every 15 seconds for approximately 1 minute.
10. Remove from the heat, toss through the spring onion leaves and serve immediately.

Serves 4

PAN-FRIED TANDOORI FISH

2 x 200 g fish fillets (I prefer Nile perch, kingklip or tuna)

1 Tbsp curry powder or 1 tsp ground cumin mixed with 1 tsp ground coriander

¼ tsp red chilli powder

¼ tsp ground turmeric

1 Tbsp tandoori masala

¼ tsp garam masala

2 Tbsp lemon or lime juice

¼ tsp salt

2 Tbsp water

1 Tbsp oil, plus extra for frying

1. Wash the fish fillets and pat dry with paper towel.
2. Combine the rest of the ingredients to make a thin paste and use this to coat the fish fillets. Marinate in a bowl in the fridge for 30 minutes. Bring to room temperature before frying.
3. Heat a little oil in a frying pan over medium heat and fry the marinated fish fillets for 4 minutes on each side or until they start looking a bit crispy. The cooking time will depend on the thickness of the fillets.
4. Serve with a vegetable side of your choice and coriander chutney (see page 121).

Serves 2

SAMAKI WA KUPAKA
[BARBECUED WHOLE FISH IN COCONUT SAUCE]

500 g whole fish (with head and tail)
1 Tbsp garlic paste
½ Tbsp ginger paste
3 Tbsp lemon or lime juice
½ tsp salt
½ tsp red chilli powder
½ tsp habanero chilli paste (optional)
¼ tsp ground turmeric
¼ tsp ground black pepper
2 Tbsp oil

COCONUT SAUCE

1 tomato, chopped
½ red onion, chopped
1 tsp garlic paste
½ tsp green chilli paste
¼ tsp ground turmeric
½ tsp ground cumin
¼ tsp curry powder
1 Tbsp oil
1 cup light coconut milk
1 cup heavy coconut milk
salt to taste
¼ tsp lemon or lime juice

1. Wash the whole fish well and remove the scales. Slit open the abdomen from the bottom and scoop out the innards. Make deep incisions all over the fish to allow the marinade to seep in.
2. In a small bowl, mix the garlic paste, ginger paste, lemon or lime juice, salt, red chilli powder, habanero chilli paste (if using), turmeric and black pepper. Use this to coat the fish well, rubbing some of the marinade into the incisions. Leave to marinate for approximately 30 minutes in the fridge.
3. To make the coconut sauce, combine the tomato, onion, garlic paste, green chilli paste, turmeric, cumin and curry powder in a blender and blend into a thick paste.
4. In a saucepan, heat the oil over medium heat, add the blended tomato paste and simmer for approximately 2 minutes. Add the light coconut milk and cook until it starts to bubble, stirring frequently.
5. Add the heavy coconut milk, season with salt and stir until it bubbles. Remove from the heat and stir in the lemon or lime juice.
6. Heat an outdoor grill to very hot and grease the grill grate with some of the oil. Place the marinated fish on the grill and cook for 10–12 minutes on each side, turning and basting with the oil until cooked through. Remove from the grill and coat the fish with the coconut sauce. Serve with steamed rice or chapattis and any remaining sauce on the side.

Serves 2

Samaki wa kupaka (barbecued whole fish in coconut sauce)

GARLIC BUTTER PRAWNS

3 Tbsp butter
½ cup chopped garlic
500 g medium prawns, cleaned and deveined
1 Tbsp coarsely ground black pepper
¼ cup chopped fresh parsley

1. In a deep frying pan, melt the butter over medium heat and sauté the garlic until fragrant, making sure it does not brown.
2. Add the prawns and turn up the heat to high. Cook for 2–3 minutes, tossing gently with a spatula to ensure even cooking.
3. Add the black pepper and cook for another 2 minutes or until the prawns turn orange, tossing every minute. Total cooking time for prawns is usually 4–5 minutes. Overcooking will change the texture of the prawns and make them chewy.
4. Add the parsley and give it a final gentle toss. Serve immediately.

NOTE: To devein prawns, use a knife to slit the back of the prawn just enough so that you can pull out the vein (it's actually the intestinal tract) that is very visible. This is crucial to avoid any kind of gastric upset from eating the prawns.

Serves 2–4

Tanzania boasts a large variety of seafood, making seafood restaurants along the coast highly popular with both tourists and locals. Growing up in a coastal city, I had the opportunity to learn from watching live seafood cooking stations, commonly found in restaurants, beach clubs and street stalls. Over the years I was able to understand the different preparation and cooking techniques associated with the different kinds of seafood. This is one of the most-loved seafood dishes among my friends and family. So simple, taking minutes to prepare and using just a few easily available ingredients, it makes for a scrumptious lunch or dinner-party starter.

CRISPY-FRIED JUMBO CHILLI PRAWNS

500 g large prawns, cleaned, peeled and deveined, and tails removed
1 Tbsp garlic paste
1 tsp paprika
3 Tbsp lemon or lime juice
¾ tsp salt

3 Tbsp cake flour or all-purpose white flour
3 Tbsp cornflour
½ tsp ground black pepper
2 tsp chopped fresh red chilli or 2 tsp dried red chilli flakes
3 cups oil

1. Place the prawns in a large mixing bowl with the garlic paste, paprika, lemon or lime juice and ¼ tsp of the salt. Mix well and allow to marinate at room temperature for 20 minutes.

2. In a separate clean bowl, combine the flour, cornflour, black pepper and fresh chilli or chilli flakes with the remaining ½ tsp salt to make a dry batter.

3. Heat the oil in a deep saucepan over medium to high heat, but not too hot.

4. Evenly coat the marinated prawns in the dry batter, one at a time, and gently drop them in the oil to deep-fry for 1–2 minutes. If using medium prawns, deep-fry for no more than a minute.

5. Serve with lemon wedges and sweet chilli sauce or your favourite dip.

Serves 2–4

Samaki is Kiswahili for fish. Many forms of cutlets are made across the region, but the main ingredient is usually potato. No part of the fish is wasted, so many families use the fishtail meat to make these.

KATLESI ZA SAMAKI [FISH CUTLETS]

¼–½ tsp salt
250 g fish (use a fillet that does not contain too
    many bones)
250 g potatoes, peeled and quartered
1 tsp garlic paste
¼ tsp ground turmeric
½ tsp green chilli paste or 2 fresh green chillies,
    finely chopped (optional)

¼ cup chopped fresh coriander
2 tsp lemon or lime juice
2 eggs
2 Tbsp fresh breadcrumbs
1½ cups oil
lemon wedges and fresh mint for serving

1. In a saucepan, bring 1 cup of water to the boil with ¼ tsp salt. Add the fish and boil for 6–8 minutes. Drain and flake the fish, making sure there are no bones.
2. In another saucepan, boil the potatoes in salted water until cooked. Drain and mash the potatoes.
3. In a bowl, combine the flaked fish and mashed potatoes with the garlic paste, turmeric, chilli (if using), coriander and lemon or lime juice.
4. Roll the mixture into balls using your hands and flatten them to make cutlets the size of your palm.
5. Beat the eggs with a pinch of salt in a small bowl, and sprinkle the breadcrumbs onto a plate.
6. Dip the cutlets in the egg and then coat in the breadcrumbs.
7. Heat the oil in a frying pan over medium heat and shallow-fry the crumbed cutlets until golden brown.
8. Serve with lemon wedges and fresh mint.

Serves 2–4

GRILLED TANDOORI PRAWN SKEWERS

500 g large prawns, cleaned, peeled and deveined
    (you can leave the tails on)
½ tsp salt
2 tsp garlic paste
1 tsp ginger paste
pinch of ground turmeric
1 tsp ground coriander
1 tsp ground cumin

1 tsp red chilli powder
1 Tbsp tandoori masala
1 Tbsp Greek yoghurt
2 Tbsp lemon or lime juice
2 Tbsp oil
2 Tbsp melted butter
fresh coriander and lemon cheeks for serving

1. Place the prawns in a bowl and sprinkle with the salt.
2. In a separate large bowl, combine the garlic paste, ginger paste, turmeric, coriander, cumin, red chilli powder, tandoori masala, Greek yoghurt, lemon or lime juice and oil.
3. Add the prawns and coat well, and allow to marinate in the fridge for 30 minutes. Bring the prawns to room temperature before cooking.
4. Heat an outdoor grill to medium hot. If using a gas barbecue, heat to 180 °C.
5. Thread the prawns onto skewers and place on the grill. Cook, turning and basting with the melted butter every 2 minutes, for a maximum of 8 minutes. Remove the prawns from the heat when they turn an opaque orange-white or pink-white colour. Prawns tend to appear curled when overcooked.
6. Drizzle with melted butter and serve with fresh coriander and lemon cheeks.

Serves 2

PRAWNS THERMIDOR

2 Tbsp butter
3 Tbsp cake flour or all-purpose white flour
3 cups full-cream milk
1½ cups grated mozzarella cheese
500 g small prawns, cleaned, peeled and deveined

1 Tbsp green chilli paste (optional)
1 Tbsp garlic paste
½ tsp salt
1 Tbsp lemon or lime juice
1½ cups water

1. In a saucepan, melt the butter over low heat and add the flour. Stir and cook for 1 minute or until well combined. Take the saucepan off the heat and gradually add the milk, stirring continuously with a whisk and making sure there are no lumps.

2. Return the saucepan to medium heat and bring the milk to the boil, stirring it with a whisk until it is thick enough to coat the back of a spoon. Turn off the heat and add ½ cup of the cheese. Combine well, then let the sauce rest, allowing the cheese to melt.

3. Place the prawns in a bowl with the green chilli paste (if using), garlic paste, salt and lemon or lime juice. Mix well and leave to marinate for 15 minutes at room temperature.

4. Preheat the oven to 230 °C.

5. In a separate clean saucepan, bring the water and marinated prawns to the boil. Boil over medium heat for 5 minutes, stirring once every minute to ensure the prawns do not stick to the bottom of the pan.

6. Using a slotted spoon, transfer the prawns to the saucepan containing the cheese sauce and mix well. Stir in 2 Tbsp of the prawn cooking liquid for added flavour.

7. Transfer the creamy prawns to an ovenproof dish, sprinkle over the rest of the cheese and bake for 15 minutes or until the cheese starts to brown. Garnish as desired.

Serves 2

Mchuzi wa dengu (lentils infused with cumin and ginger)

Vegetables

A staple in India and Pakistan, lentils of varying types and in varying forms are consumed all across East Africa. An interesting fact is that Tanzania actually exports lentils to India! This delicious daal (also spelt dal, dhal or dahl) makes a filling main served with rice.

MCHUZI WA DENGU
[LENTILS INFUSED WITH CUMIN AND GINGER]

1 cup yellow lentils, soaked overnight
5 cups water
¼ tsp ground turmeric
1 large ripe tomato, halved
1 tsp salt
1 tsp garlic paste
1 tsp ground coriander

¼ cup oil
1 Tbsp thinly sliced ginger
3 fresh green chillies, halved lengthwise
1 Tbsp cumin seeds
1 large red onion, finely chopped
2 Tbsp chopped fresh coriander
crispy fried onion for garnishing (optional)

1. Rinse the lentils and place them in a large saucepan with the water, turmeric, tomato halves and ½ tsp of the salt. Bring to the boil and boil for approximately 25 minutes until the lentils are soft, making sure they do not cook dry. If needed, add an additional cup of water. Once cooked, remove from the heat and stir using a whisk. Remove any large tomato peel. Stir in the garlic paste and ground coriander, return to the heat and simmer over low heat for approximately 5 minutes. Set aside.

2. In a large deep saucepan, heat the oil and fry the ginger and chillies for 30 seconds. Add the cumin seeds and fry for approximately 15 seconds or until fragrant. Add the onion and sauté until it just begins to brown. Remove from the heat immediately.

3. Add the lentils to the tempered spices – you will hear a sizzle. Mix well and transfer to a serving dish. Garnish with the chopped fresh coriander and crispy fried onion (if using), and serve with rice, chapattis or a bread of your choice.

NOTES: Lentils cook faster if they are left to soak overnight.

Tempering (or briefly toasting) involves sizzling the whole spices in hot oil until they crackle. This helps to release their flavours and beautiful aromas, and enhances the overall flavour of the dish.

Serves 4

This delicious kidney bean curry belongs to the list of Tanzania's unique foods. Popular in the western part of the country, it is a nutritious staple in most Swahili homes. This recipe allows you to substitute tinned coconut milk or cream for fresh coconut milk, which can be time-consuming to prepare and depends on the availability of coconuts.

MCHUZI WA MAHARAGE
[RED KIDNEY BEAN COCONUT CURRY]

2 cups fresh or tinned red kidney beans
2 tomatoes, grated
¼ tsp ground turmeric
½ tsp garlic paste
½ tsp green chilli paste or chopped fresh green chilli
2 tsp ground coriander

¼ tsp salt
1 Tbsp oil
1 red onion, finely chopped
3 cups fresh or tinned coconut milk, or coconut cream
¼ cup roughly chopped fresh coriander

1. If using fresh kidney beans, boil in a saucepan of salted water for 25 minutes or until cooked (avoid overcooking). Drain and set aside. If using tinned kidney beans, drain the liquid, rinse with fresh water to remove excess salt and set aside.
2. In a bowl, combine the tomatoes, turmeric, garlic paste, chilli paste or fresh chilli, ground coriander and salt.
3. Heat the oil in a saucepan over medium to high heat and sauté the onion until translucent.
4. Add the tomato mixture and give it a good stir. Cover the saucepan with a lid and cook for 1–2 minutes.
5. Add the kidney beans and stir gently to avoid mashing them up.
6. Add the coconut milk or cream and chopped fresh coriander. Stir gently and cook until the curry starts to bubble. Remove from the heat immediately.
7. Serve with rice or chapattis.

Serves 2

Zanzibar mix is one of the most popular street foods in Dar es Salaam and Zanzibar. It is usually prepared using fresh coconut milk, but my version allows for it to be enjoyed in parts of the world where making fresh coconut milk is either impossible or very time-consuming, without compromising on any of the absolutely exotic and complex flavours of this famous Zanzibari dish!

ZANZIBAR MIX
[CHICKPEAS AND POTATOES IN COCONUT MILK]

500 g potatoes, washed
50 g black chickpeas, soaked overnight
½ Tbsp water
1 tsp green chilli paste
¼ tsp ground turmeric
1 Tbsp oil
pinch of black mustard seeds

¼ tsp garlic paste
2 x 400 ml tins light coconut milk
2 x 400 ml tins heavy coconut milk
½ tsp salt
2 tsp lemon or lime juice
fresh coriander for garnishing

1. Boil the whole, unpeeled potatoes in a saucepan of salted water until just done. Allow to cool, then peel and dice into 2.5 cm cubes.
2. Drain the chickpeas and boil in a separate saucepan of salted water until cooked through. Drain any excess water.
3. In a small bowl, mix the water, green chilli paste and turmeric.
4. Heat the oil in a large saucepan over medium heat and temper the mustard seeds for approximately 15 seconds. Add the chilli and turmeric paste and give it a good stir. Add the garlic paste, cooked chickpeas and potato cubes and stir well.
5. Lower the heat and pour in the light coconut milk. Stir well and simmer until the coconut milk just starts to bubble.
6. Add the heavy coconut milk and salt and stir until the mixture starts to bubble. Remove from the heat and add the lemon or lime juice. Give it a final stir and serve, garnished with fresh coriander.

NOTE: You can add toppings such as crushed bhajia za kunde (black-eyed pea fritters, see page 132) and salted potato crisps.

Serves 4

Cabbage is one of the most popular vegetables across East Africa, and is consumed in a variety of ways – in soups, salads, appetisers and main dishes. This recipe is versatile because it can be served as a side dish or as a main, especially if you are a fan of this leafy vegetable. I have added carrots to give the dish some colour, texture and added flavour.

KABICHI YA KUKAANGA
[CABBAGE STIR-FRY]

3 Tbsp oil
1 red onion, chopped
1 tsp garlic paste
1 habanero chilli pepper, chopped (optional)
½ carrot, peeled and grated

½ tsp salt
¼ tsp red chilli powder
¼ large cabbage, thinly sliced
1 Tbsp tomato purée

1. Heat the oil in a large saucepan over medium to high heat and sauté the onion until translucent.
2. Turn down the heat to medium and add the garlic paste and habanero chilli pepper (if using).
3. Cook for 1 minute, stirring continuously, then add the carrot and cook for a further 2 minutes.
4. Season with the salt and red chilli powder and mix well.
5. Add the cabbage and tomato purée and combine well with the rest of the ingredients. Cook for 5–7 minutes to allow the cabbage to soften, stirring occasionally.

Serves 2 as a side

People in the coastal cities and towns in particular love muhogo (cassava). This recipe is popular in Zanzibar and Mombasa, and a must-have across the region during the holy month of Ramadan at Iftar (the breaking of the fast at sunset).

MUHOGO WA NAZI
[CASSAVA IN COCONUT SAUCE]

500 g cassava, peeled and cut into 5 cm cubes
pinch of ground turmeric
¼ tsp garlic paste
½ tsp salt
4 cups water
1 Tbsp oil
1 small tomato, grated

1 tsp chopped fresh green chilli
1 cup light coconut milk
1 cup heavy coconut milk
handful of chopped fresh coriander
1 tsp lemon or lime juice
sliced fresh red chilli for garnishing

1. Place the cassava, turmeric, garlic paste and ¼ tsp of the salt in a medium saucepan, cover with the water and bring to the boil. Boil until the cassava becomes soft. Drain any excess water and set aside.
2. In another large saucepan, heat the oil over medium heat and sauté the tomato and chilli for approximately 2 minutes.
3. Add the light coconut milk and cooked cassava. Turn down the heat and simmer for 10 minutes or until the coconut milk starts to bubble.
4. Add the heavy coconut milk, the remaining salt and half of the coriander. Simmer for 5 minutes, stirring occasionally, until the coconut milk thickens.
5. Add the lemon or lime juice, mix well and simmer for 1 minute.
6. Remove from the heat and garnish with the remaining coriander and sliced fresh red chilli.

Serves 2

CHEESY VEGETABLE AND PASTA BAKE

200 g penne pasta
1 cup fresh or tinned sweet corn kernels
1 cup chopped fresh or tinned green beans
½ cup fresh or tinned peas
2 heaped Tbsp butter
3 Tbsp cake flour or all-purpose white flour
3 cups full-cream milk
1 cup grated Cheddar cheese
¼ tsp coarsely ground black pepper
½ tsp dried origanum

½ tsp dried red chilli flakes
¾ tsp salt
2 Tbsp oil
1 Tbsp garlic paste
1 red or white onion, chopped
1 carrot, peeled and chopped
½ green bell pepper, deseeded and chopped
1 cup grated mozzarella cheese
fresh herbs for garnishing

1. Bring a saucepan of lightly salted water to the boil. Add the pasta and boil for approximately 9 minutes or until al dente. Drain and set aside.

2. If using fresh sweet corn kernels and green beans, blanch them before proceeding – they must feel firm to the touch. Similarly, boil fresh peas until cooked. If using tinned ingredients, drain the liquid before measuring.

3. In another saucepan, melt the butter over medium heat and mix in the flour. Cook for 30 seconds or until well incorporated. Remove from the heat and gradually add the milk, stirring continuously with a whisk to ensure there are no lumps.

4. Return the saucepan to medium heat and bring to the boil, stirring until thick enough to coat the back of a spoon. Turn off the heat and add the Cheddar cheese, black pepper, origanum, red chilli flakes and ¼ tsp of the salt. Mix well and allow the cheese to melt.

5. Preheat the oven to 220 °C.

6. Heat the oil in a frying pan over medium heat and sauté the garlic paste until fragrant, making sure it does not brown, then add the onion and sauté for 1 minute.

7. Add the sweet corn kernels, green beans, peas, carrot and remaining salt and sauté for approximately 2 minutes. Add the bell pepper and sauté for approximately 1 minute. Remove from the heat.

8. Pour the cheese sauce into the frying pan containing the vegetables. Add the cooked pasta and mix well.

9. Transfer the mixture to an ovenproof dish and sprinkle over the mozzarella cheese. Bake for 8–10 minutes or until the cheese starts to brown.

10. Garnish with fresh herbs of your choice.

Serves 4

GRILLED CHEESE, VEGETABLE AND CORIANDER SANDWICHES

2 potatoes
8 slices bread of your choice
butter for spreading and grilling
½ cucumber, peeled and thinly sliced
2 tomatoes, thinly sliced
1 red or white onion, sliced
½ cup grated mozzarella cheese
salt to taste

CORIANDER CHUTNEY

3 cups fresh coriander
¼ cup almonds
¼ cup cashew nuts, roasted
5 fresh green chillies or ½ Tbsp green chilli paste
¼ tsp salt
1 tsp lemon or lime juice
¼ cup water

1. To make the coriander chutney, place all the ingredients in a blender and blend until the mixture is smooth enough to spread. Set aside.
2. Wash the potatoes and boil them in their skins in a saucepan of salted water for approximately 20 minutes until soft. Pierce them with a skewer or knife to test whether they are cooked. Drain all the water and let the potatoes cool down until they are easy to handle. Peel off their skins and slice thinly.
3. Remove the crusts (optional) and butter the bread. Spread coriander chutney on each slice.
4. To build your sandwiches, layer the cucumber, tomato, onion and potato slices on top of the coriander chutney. Sprinkle the cheese over the potatoes, season with salt and close the sandwiches.
5. Lightly brush a frying or griddle pan with butter. Gently place the sandwiches in the pan and toast for 1 minute on each side to allow the cheese to melt. Alternatively, use a sandwich maker or press.
6. Serve the sandwiches with the remaining coriander chutney on the side.

NOTE: This coriander chutney is quite spicy, but you can tweak the amount of chilli to suit your tolerance. Any leftover chutney can be refrigerated for up to 1 week.

Serves 4

SPICED SCRAMBLED EGGS

1 Tbsp butter
1 red or white onion, chopped
1 tomato, chopped
1 fresh green chilli, finely chopped, or
    ¼ tsp red chilli powder

¼ tsp salt
¼ tsp ground turmeric
½ tsp ground coriander
8 eggs, beaten
fresh coriander and sliced fresh chilli for garnishing

1. In a deep frying pan, melt the butter over medium to high heat and sauté the onion until translucent.
2. Add the tomato, fresh chilli or chilli powder and salt and mix well. Cook for approximately 1 minute.
3. Add the turmeric and coriander and mix well. Cook for 1 minute.
4. Pour in the beaten eggs and swirl using a spatula until the eggs appear just cooked (avoid drying them out).
5. Serve on buttered slices of your favourite bread, garnished with fresh coriander and sliced fresh chilli.

Serves 2–4

This common Zanzibari dish made with large-leaf spinach makes a super nutritious accompaniment. The combination of tomatoes and coconut cream reduces the bitterness of the mchicha, which is basically the East African cousin of traditional spinach.

MCHICHA WA NAZI
[SPINACH IN COCONUT SAUCE]

250 g large-leaf spinach
2 Tbsp oil
1 red onion, finely chopped
1 tsp garlic paste
2 large tomatoes, grated
¼ tsp red chilli powder (optional)
½ tsp ground coriander

½ tsp salt
2 tsp tomato purée
½ cup coconut cream
1 habanero chilli pepper or any fresh chilli of your choice, chopped
fresh coriander for garnishing
extra sliced fresh chillies for garnishing

1. Wash the spinach and chop the leaves together with the stems.
2. Heat the oil in a saucepan over medium heat and sauté the onion and garlic paste until the onion appears translucent. Add the tomatoes, cover the saucepan with a lid and cook for 3 minutes.
3. Add the red chilli powder (if using), coriander, salt and tomato purée. Mix well and simmer for 1 minute.
4. Add the spinach and stir frequently for 2 minutes (the leaves will reduce in volume to less than half while cooking).
5. Stir in the coconut cream and chilli, and simmer for 4 minutes over low to medium heat until thickened. Serve immediately, garnished with fresh coriander and extra sliced fresh chillies.

Serves 4 as a side

A family favourite, these fritters are popular in Kenya, where they are known as maru bhajia. Simple to prepare, they make a perfect rainy-day snack served with a cup of hot tea. Beware: you won't be able to stop eating these once you start!

BHAJIA ZA VIAZI NA KACHUMBARI
[CRISPY POTATO FRITTERS WITH TOMATO AND ONION CHUTNEY]

4 potatoes, washed and peeled
1½ cups sifted chickpea flour (also known as gram flour or besan)
3 Tbsp rice flour
½ tsp garlic paste
¼ tsp ginger paste
½ tsp salt
¼ tsp ground cumin
1 Tbsp lemon or lime juice
pinch of ground turmeric
1 tsp green chilli paste
¼ cup chopped fresh coriander
¼ tsp red chilli powder (optional)
3 cups oil

TOMATO AND ONION CHUTNEY

2 large ripe tomatoes, grated
½ red onion, finely chopped
½ carrot, peeled and finely grated
¼ cucumber, peeled and finely grated
¼ tsp garlic paste
1 Tbsp lemon or lime juice
2 Tbsp finely chopped fresh coriander
¼ tsp green chilli paste
salt to taste

1. Slice the potatoes to a thickness of 0.5 cm.
2. To make the chutney, mix all the ingredients in a bowl and set aside.
3. In a mixing bowl, combine the chickpea flour, rice flour, garlic paste, ginger paste, salt, cumin, lemon or lime juice, turmeric, green chilli paste, coriander and red chilli powder (if using). Mix in water as needed until you arrive at a medium thick batter (the batter should be able to coat the potato slices and not drip).
4. Heat the oil in a deep frying pan. Coat each potato slice with the batter and carefully drop into the oil, one at a time, deep-frying in batches of not more than 8–10 at a time. Fry for 2 minutes, then gently flip the potato slices and continue to fry until slightly golden brown.
5. Serve hot with the tomato and onion chutney.

NOTE: You can make rice flour by simply grinding long-grain rice into a fine powder.

Serves 2–3

GREEN LENTILS INFUSED WITH CURRY LEAVES

2 cups green lentils, soaked overnight
4 cups water
1 tsp salt
2 Tbsp oil
1 tsp yellow or black mustard seeds
5 dried curry leaves
1 red onion, finely chopped
3 large tomatoes, blended
2 tsp tomato purée or paste
2 tsp garlic paste

2 tsp curry powder
1 tsp ground cumin
1 tsp ground coriander
½ tsp red chilli powder
¼ tsp ground turmeric
1 tsp lemon or lime juice
¼ cup fresh coriander
fresh curry leaves (optional)
sliced fresh red chilli for garnishing

1. Rinse the lentils and place them in a large saucepan with the water and ½ tsp of the salt. Cover the saucepan with a lid, bring to the boil and boil for 15 minutes. Lower the heat and simmer the lentils, uncovered, for a further 10 minutes, making sure they do not cook dry. If needed, add more water. Once cooked, drain the lentils and reserve the liquid.

2. In another saucepan, heat the oil over medium heat and add the mustard seeds and curry leaves. Temper the spices for 15 seconds to help release their flavour and aroma. Keep a distance while tempering, as mustard seeds have a tendency to crackle out of the pan.

3. Add the onion and sauté until translucent.

4. Add the tomatoes, tomato purée or paste, garlic paste, curry powder, cumin, ground coriander, red chilli powder, turmeric and remaining salt. Cover the saucepan with a lid and simmer for approximately 3 minutes.

5. Add the cooked lentils and ¼ cup of the reserved liquid and mix well. Reduce the heat to low and add the lemon or lime juice. Simmer for a further 5 minutes. Garnish with the fresh coriander and curry leaves (if using) and sliced fresh chilli before serving.

Serves 4

EGG AND VEGETABLE STUFFED CHAPATTIS

¼ cup oil
2 red onions, chopped
¼ tsp garlic paste
2 carrots, peeled and grated
1 cup thinly shredded cabbage
¼ cup finely chopped green bell pepper
1 tsp chopped fresh green chilli
pinch of ground turmeric
¼ tsp ground cumin
¼ tsp salt
2 Tbsp chopped fresh coriander
3 eggs

CHAPATTI DOUGH

2 cups sifted cake flour or all-purpose white flour
½ tsp salt
3 Tbsp oil
½ cup warm water

1. Heat 2 Tbsp of the oil in a frying pan over medium heat and sauté the onions until translucent.
2. Add the garlic paste, stir and cook for 1 minute.
3. Add the carrots and sauté for approximately 2 minutes.
4. Add the cabbage, bell pepper and chilli followed by the turmeric, cumin and salt. Stir well and cook for 2–3 minutes over medium to high heat.
5. Add the coriander, stir well and remove from the heat. Set aside to cool to room temperature.
6. Once cool, add the eggs and stir well using a fork.
7. To make the dough, combine all the ingredients in a mixing bowl and knead for approximately 15 minutes, gradually adding more water if needed. The dough should be slightly soft, smooth to the touch and stretchy. Cover the bowl with a damp cloth and allow the dough to rest for 20 minutes at room temperature.
8. Grease your fingertips with some oil, divide the dough into 4 portions and roll into smooth balls using your hands. Dust your work surface with some flour and, using a rolling pin, roll the dough into very thin, roughly 20 cm squares. It is essential that the dough is thinly rolled, as this will allow the heat to penetrate into the stuffing and cook the eggs.
9. Spoon the egg and vegetable filling onto the centre of each square and fold in the sides to create a parcel, ensuring there are no gaps for the filling to spill out.
10. In a frying pan, heat ½ Tbsp of the remaining oil over low heat. Gently place a stuffed chapatti in the pan and cook on one side until it starts to brown, then turn over and cook the other side. Flip over and cook the first side again, gently pressing down on the chapatti with the back of the spatula to ensure the stuffing is as close to the heat as possible. Cook until golden brown, then turn over and brown the other side.
11. Repeat with the remaining 3 stuffed chapattis, using ½ Tbsp oil to cook each one.

Serves 4

These delicious fritters are enjoyed across East Africa. They make a great teatime snack with a side of coconut chutney, but are also enjoyed as part of a breakfast meal at local teashops.

BHAJIA ZA KUNDE
[BLACK-EYED PEA FRITTERS]

250 g black-eyed peas, soaked overnight
1 red onion, chopped
3 fresh green chillies, chopped
1 cup chopped fresh coriander

¼ cup water
1 tsp garlic paste
1 tsp salt
3 cups oil

1. Using your hands, gently rub the soaked black-eyed peas to remove any shells. Drain and rinse.
2. Place the black-eyed peas, red onion, green chillies, coriander and water in a blender or food processor. Blend on high speed until thick and creamy (avoid over-blending, the mixture must not be runny). You may add extra water while blending, 1 Tbsp at a time, if necessary.
3. Transfer the mixture to a mixing bowl and add the garlic paste and salt. Using a fork, gently whip the mixture for 30 seconds.
4. Heat the oil in a deep frying pan over medium heat. Gently drop spoonfuls of the mixture into the oil and fry until the fritters are brown and crispy. Drain on paper towel.
5. Serve hot with chutney or a sauce of your choice.

NOTE: You can prepare the mixture (without the garlic paste and salt) and leave it in the fridge, covered, for up to 6 hours before frying. Bring it to room temperature before frying.

Serves 4 as a snack

These delicious, tangy potato balls are very simple to prepare and make a great party snack served with a variety of chutneys and dips. Found on teashop menus as a vegetarian starter, kachori are an absolute favourite in the region.

SWAHILI KACHORI
[FRIED DUMPLINGS]

5 large potatoes
¼ tsp garlic paste
¼ tsp salt
pinch of ground turmeric
¼ tsp red chilli powder
2 tsp lemon or lime juice
handful of chopped fresh coriander
2 cups oil

BATTER
1 cup chickpea flour (also known as gram flour
   or besan)
¼ tsp salt
pinch of red chilli powder
1 Tbsp chopped fresh coriander
½ cup water

1. Wash the potatoes and boil them in their skins in a saucepan of lightly salted water for approximately 20 minutes until soft. Pierce them with a skewer or knife to test whether they are cooked.
2. Drain all the water and let the potatoes cool down until they are easy to handle. Peel off their skins and then mash the potatoes in a mixing bowl.
3. Add the garlic paste, salt, turmeric, red chilli powder, lemon or lime juice and coriander. Using a spatula, mix until evenly combined.
4. Using your hands, form the mixture into smooth balls roughly 5 cm in diameter.
5. In a separate clean bowl, mix all the ingredients for the batter.
6. Dip each of the balls in the batter, making sure they are evenly coated.
7. Heat the oil in a deep frying pan over medium to high heat. Gently drop the batter-coated balls into the oil and fry until golden. Cook a maximum of 2 to 3 at a time. Drain on paper towel.

Serves 4 as a snack

Chapatti is a common type of flatbread found across East Africa. It comes in different forms and is often eaten as a side with curry. While it originated in India where it is made with whole-wheat flour, across Africa it is generally made with white flour.

EAST AFRICAN CHAPATTIS

2 cups sifted cake flour or all-purpose white flour or whole-wheat flour
½ tsp salt

3 Tbsp oil (you will need about 6 Tbsp extra for frying)
½ cup warm water

1. Combine the flour, salt, oil and water in a mixing bowl and knead for approximately 15 minutes, gradually adding more water if needed. The dough should be slightly soft, smooth to the touch and stretchy. Cover the bowl with a damp cloth and allow the dough to rest for 20 minutes at room temperature.
2. Grease your hands with some oil to prevent the dough from sticking to them. Transfer the dough to a floured work surface and knead for another 5 minutes. Divide the dough into 6 portions and allow to rest for another 15 minutes.
3. Using a rolling pin, roll each portion into a circle of up to 18 cm in diameter.
4. Heat a non-stick frying pan or crêpe pan over medium to high heat. Smear with ½ Tbsp oil and place a chapatti in the pan. Cook for 30 seconds and then smear the chapatti with ½ Tbsp oil before turning over to cook the other side. Cook for approximately 2 minutes, turning as needed until both sides are light brown. Repeat with the rest of the chapattis.

Makes 6

My absolute favourite, the pungent flavours of black mustard seeds and freshly squeezed lemon or lime juice make these potatoes extremely delicious. This accompaniment adds fiery flavour to the tamest of meals!

VIAZI MASALA
[FLAMING-HOT POTATOES]

250 g potatoes
1 Tbsp oil
1 tsp black mustard seeds
¼ tsp ground turmeric
¼ cup tomato purée or paste

1 tsp red chilli powder
¼ tsp salt
1 tsp ground cumin
½ cup water
2 tsp lemon or lime juice

1. Wash the potatoes and boil them in their skins in a saucepan of salted water for approximately 20 minutes until soft. Pierce them with a skewer or knife to test whether they are cooked.
2. Drain all the water and let the potatoes cool down until they are easy to handle. Peel off their skins and dice into 5 cm cubes.
3. In a separate saucepan, heat the oil over medium heat and add the mustard seeds. Let the seeds crackle for approximately 30 seconds.
4. Add the turmeric, tomato purée or paste, red chilli powder, salt, cumin and water. Mix well, cover the saucepan with a lid and simmer for 3 minutes.
5. Add the diced potatoes and stir gently. Add the lemon or lime juice and stir again. Simmer, covered, for another minute over low heat.

Serves 4 as a side

This is a family favourite on Sunday mornings with a side of eggs and a loaf of white bread. Invented by my great-grandmother in the early 1900s, a few years after she migrated with her husband to Tanzania, this warm dipping chutney is a hit with my family and friends.

TOMATO CHUTNEY

2 Tbsp oil
6 large ripe tomatoes, chopped into 2.5 cm cubes
1 tsp garlic paste
¼ tsp ground turmeric
1 Tbsp curry powder

1 tsp red chilli powder
½ tsp salt
½ cup roughly chopped fresh coriander
½ cup water

1. Heat the oil in a saucepan over medium heat. Add the tomatoes, garlic paste, turmeric, curry powder, red chilli powder and salt. Mix using a spatula, cover the saucepan with a lid and simmer for 3–4 minutes.
2. Stir in the coriander and water and simmer, covered, for approximately 10 minutes or until the tomatoes are tender. The chutney should be quite runny.
3. Serve with soft warm bread or chapattis. Store any leftovers in the fridge for up to 48 hours.

Serves 2

Sweet vermicelli milk pudding

Desserts

This dessert is popular in all East African countries, especially during Ramadan, when a variety of foods are presented every evening to break the fast. This sweet vermicelli is almost certain to be among the multiple dessert options served daily during the holy month.

SWEET VERMICELLI MILK PUDDING

250 g vermicelli, broken up
1 Tbsp unsalted butter
¾ cup white sugar
1 tsp ground cardamom
1½ cups heavy coconut milk

¼ cup evaporated milk
¼ cup pistachios, roughly chopped
¼ cup almonds, roughly chopped
1 Tbsp pomegranate seeds (optional)
edible flowers

1. Bring a medium saucepan of water to the boil, add the vermicelli and parboil for 2–3 minutes. Drain and set aside.

2. Melt the butter in a heavy-bottomed saucepan over low heat. Add the parboiled vermicelli and mix well.

3. Add the sugar and cardamom and mix well.

4. Gradually pour in the coconut milk followed by the evaporated milk, stirring gently at the same time. Avoid mashing the vermicelli.

5. Turn up the heat to medium and simmer the milk for 3–4 minutes. Remove from the heat once the milk starts to bubble.

6. Allow the saucepan to cool to room temperature, then refrigerate for a minimum of 1 hour before serving in bowls. Garnish with the nuts, pomegranate seeds (if using) and edible flowers.

Serves 4

Typically a breakfast snack, this Swahili version of a fried bun is found on every street corner and breakfast table across East Africa, more so along the coast. Whether dipped in milky tea or served with strong spiced black tea, mandazi is a must-have at chai time!

MANDAZI

250 g cake flour or all-purpose white flour, sifted
100 g white or brown sugar
½ Tbsp instant dry yeast

1 tsp ground cardamom
oil
¾ cup coconut milk or lukewarm full-cream milk

1. Place the flour, sugar, yeast, cardamom and 2 Tbsp oil in a mixing bowl. Combine well.
2. Add the milk, a little at a time, to form a dough (you may not need all the milk). Knead for approximately 10 minutes until the dough is soft to the touch.
3. Cover the bowl with a tea towel and leave for approximately 45 minutes, until the dough has doubled in size.
4. Transfer the risen dough to a flat, floured surface and roll it into a smooth ball with your hands. Using a sharp knife, divide the dough into 4 portions and roll into balls.
5. Using a rolling pin, roll the balls into circles 2.5 cm thick and 5–6 cm in diameter. Slice the circles into quarters.
6. Heat 2 cups oil in a large deep frying pan over medium to high heat. Place the dough triangles in the pan and fry for approximately 1 minute, gently splashing oil on the tops to help them puff up. Turn them over and fry for approximately 1 minute on the other side. If using a smaller frying pan, fry a maximum of 3 triangles at a time to get perfectly risen mandazi. Drain on paper towel.

Serves 4 (makes 16)

Many versions of these doughnuts exist, but my version uses two of my favourite Zanzibari spices – cardamom and cinnamon – to give it a more authentic island flavour. This is the perfect snack to have during the rainy season with a hot cup of tea.

MINI DOUGHNUTS

1 cup sifted cake flour or all-purpose white flour
¼ cup brown sugar
½ tsp ground cardamom
¼ tsp ground cinnamon

½ cup lukewarm full-cream milk
1 tsp baking powder
2 cups oil

1. In a mixing bowl, combine the flour, sugar, cardamom and cinnamon.
2. Gradually add the lukewarm milk, stirring at the same time, to form a thick batter. Set the batter aside for 15 minutes.
3. Add the baking powder and stir well.
4. Heat the oil in a deep frying pan over medium to high heat. Gently drop spoonfuls of the batter into the oil and fry until golden brown. Drain on paper towel.

Serves 2–4 (makes 8–10)

A delicacy for coconut lovers, kashata ya nazi is a favourite dessert in many East African homes. Use desiccated coconut if fresh is not available.

KASHATA YA NAZI
[COCONUT CANDY]

200 g grated fresh coconut (see step 1)
100 g white sugar
1 Tbsp butter
1 Tbsp evaporated or regular full-cream milk

1 tsp ground cardamom
½ tsp red food colouring (optional)
handful of chopped or whole nuts (cashews, almonds or pistachios)

1. Crack one large coconut and use a knife to separate the white flesh from the shell. You can either use a grater to grate the flesh or place the chopped pieces in a food processor and pulse until you arrive at a finely grated texture.

2. Place all the ingredients, except the nuts, in a heavy-bottomed saucepan and cook over medium heat for 15 minutes, stirring continuously until the mixture thickens. It should almost resemble a soft ball of dough.

3. Line a baking tray or heatproof board with baking paper. Transfer the thickened mixture to the paper and use a rolling pin or spatula to spread it to your desired thickness. Score into squares (or any shape you fancy) using a sharp knife.

4. Gently press the whole or chopped nuts into the mixture and allow to set at room temperature for 5–6 hours. Once the squares have set (semi-hard), you can slice them all the way through.

Serves 4 (makes 8)

East Africa is known for its variety of plantain bananas, my favourite being the sweet plantains. When mixed with spices, plantains create flavour-bursting dishes. These sweet plantain fritters are very easy to make and are a great festive dessert. The plantains maintain their firmness and sweetness when deep-fried.

TUMBUA NDIZI
[SWEET PLANTAIN FRITTERS]

250 g cake flour or all-purpose white flour, sifted
½ cup white sugar
1¼ tsp ground cardamom
1 cup heavy coconut milk

1 tsp baking powder
3 ripe sweet plantains
2 cups oil

1. In a large mixing bowl, combine the flour, sugar, cardamom and coconut milk. Stir and leave the batter to thicken at room temperature for 2 hours.
2. Add the baking powder and mix well.
3. Peel the plantains and cut in half. Slice each half lengthwise to make 4 portions per plantain.
4. Heat the oil over high heat, dip the plantain portions into the batter and deep-fry until golden brown. Drain on paper towel.

Serves 2–4 (makes 12)

This nutty, textured, soft biscotti is the perfect Swahili teatime treat.
Best enjoyed with a hot cup of masala chai or coffee.

PEANUT BISCOTTI

2½ cups white sugar
1 egg
¾ cup butter, at room temperature
5 cups sifted cake flour or all-purpose white flour

2½ cups raw peanuts, skins removed, lightly roasted
and roughly chopped
2½ tsp baking powder
1 Tbsp melted butter

1. Preheat the oven to 160 °C and grease a baking tray.
2. Place the sugar, egg and butter in a mixing bowl and beat with an electric mixer for approximately 10 minutes. Switch off the mixer and add the flour, peanuts and baking powder. Use a spatula to combine well.
3. Place the dough on the greased tray and use your hands to flatten it to a thickness of 4 cm. Brush the dough with the melted butter and bake for 30 minutes.
4. Allow to cool for 10 minutes before using a flat metal spatula to lift the biscotti out of the tray. Slice into strips and store in an airtight container for up to 1 week.

Serves 4 (makes 16)

This sweet dish is available in all of the coastal regions of East Africa and comes in many forms, such as hard, soft or crumbly. This soft yet crumbly version is my favourite and perfect served with a blend of your favourite black spiced coffee, which is how it is typically enjoyed in East Africa. The stronger the coffee the better, no sugar!

KASHATA ZA KARANGA
[PEANUT BRITTLE]

300 g raw peanuts
1 cup water
¾ cup brown sugar

1 tsp ground cardamom
1 Tbsp full-cream milk

1. Preheat the oven to 175 °C. Place the peanuts on a baking tray and roast for 20 minutes. Remove the skins from the roasted peanuts and roughly chop. Set aside 25 g and grind the rest in a blender or grinder.
2. Line a baking tray or heatproof board with baking paper.
3. In a small saucepan, bring the water and sugar to the boil and simmer for 10 minutes, making sure the sugar does not burn. Use a wooden spatula to stir frequently while the texture of the syrup reduces to a slightly stringy (three-thread) consistency.
4. Reduce the heat to low and add the cardamom. Give it a quick stir and then add the milk and the ground and chopped peanuts.
5. Stir again quickly and then immediately pour the mixture onto the paper-lined tray or board and flatten out to a thickness of 2.5 cm using a rolling pin or palette knife.
6. Using a sharp knife, score the brittle into squares and allow to set for 30 minutes or until cooled to room temperature before cutting all the way through.

NOTE: The brittle will keep in an airtight container for up to 1 week.

Makes 12

Most commonly found along the beautiful coastal towns and islands, this is my favourite East African dessert. These dumplings are relished during the holy month of Ramadan, eaten in the evenings after breaking the fast, with a hot cup of tea or coffee.

KAIMATI
[SWEET DUMPLINGS]

200 g cake flour or all-purpose white flour, sifted
1 tsp ground cardamom
1 tsp instant dry yeast
1 cup lukewarm full-cream milk

3 cups oil
1¼ cups white sugar
¾ cup water

1. Place the flour, cardamom and yeast in a mixing bowl. Gradually pour in the lukewarm milk to make a very thick batter. You should be able to make an irregular-sized ball of batter using your hand. (Make sure not to turn the batter into dough.) Cover the bowl and set aside at room temperature for approximately 30 minutes or until the batter has risen.

2. Grease your hands with some oil and gently mix the risen batter.

3. Heat the oil in a deep frying pan over low to medium heat. Using your hands, pull off small portions of the batter, roll into dumplings and gently drop into the oil. Use a slotted spoon to constantly turn the dumplings to ensure even cooking. Fry until light brown in colour. (Frying over low heat ensures the batter is cooked through.) Drain the fried dumplings on a piece of baking paper.

4. Use a heavy-bottomed saucepan to make the perfect sugar syrup. First add the sugar and then the water. You will need enough water to cover the sugar in the pan. Stir over medium heat until all the sugar has dissolved and the syrup appears thick but not caramelised.

5. Pour the hot sugar syrup over the fried dumplings and immediately mix to coat.

6. Serve warm with a cup of tea or coffee.

Serves 4 (makes 16)

INDEX

METRIC TO CUPS/SPOONS

Metric	Teaspoons	Metric	Cups
2ml	¼ tsp	60ml	¼ cup
3ml	½ tsp	80ml	1/3 cup
5ml	1 tsp	125ml	½ cup
10ml	2 tsp	160ml	2/3 cup
20ml	4 tsp	200ml	¾ cup
		250ml	1 cup
Metric	Tablespoons	375ml	1½ cups
15ml	1 Tbsp	500ml	2 cups
30ml	2 Tbsp	750ml	3 cups
45ml	3 Tbsp	1 litre	4 cups
60ml	4 Tbsp		